THE HOUSE ON THE CLIFF

A Mystery Comedy

by

GEORGE BATSON

SAMUEL FRENCH

LONDON

NEW YORK   TORONTO   SYDNEY   HOLLYWOOD

CHARACTERS

(in order of their appearance)

KAREN
DOCTOR LANE   4 0
ELLEN CLAYTON
JENNY
NURSE PEPPER
COREY PHILLIPS

SYNOPSIS OF SCENES

The action of the play passes in the living-room of Cliff House, overlooking the Channel

ACT I
SCENE 1   Early afternoon in September
SCENE 2   Late afternoon, two days later

ACT II
SCENE 1   Afternoon, several days later
SCENE 2   Eight-thirty the same night

ACT III
One o'clock the following afternoon

Time—the present

ACT I

SCENE I

SCENE—*The living-room of Cliff House. September, early afternoon.*

The house is a rambling old structure of ancient vintage, built high on a cliff overlooking the Channel. The room is comfortable, well furnished, and suggests wealth. An arched opening R leads to a reception hall and the rest of the house. Up C are glass doors opening on a balcony-porch which runs along the rear of the house and overlooks the water. The balcony-porch is not wide and has an iron grille railing. In the direct centre of the railing is a small gate which leads down on the cliff to a ledge. Down L are french windows which open on a garden and the driveway. R of the windows is one section of a large bookcase which juts out. It is interrupted by a fire-place LC, with a portrait of John Clayton hanging above it. The bookcase resumes on the other side of the fireplace. Both sections reach to the ceiling and are packed with books. RC is a sofa with a coffee-table below it. A desk with a telephone on it and a chair behind it, is LC. There is room round this desk for ELLEN's wheelchair to exit through the french windows either above or below it. A chair stands LC below the desk, and a drinks table L of the porch doors up C. There is a piano up R, and a small table below the arched opening.

When the CURTAIN rises KAREN is playing passages from Rachmaninov's Second Piano Concerto. She has been a concert pianist but is in temporary retirement. She is in her thirties, tall and slim, and with a cool beauty. After a few moments she stops playing, wrings her hands, then nervously rises and paces to down C and round L of the desk to above it. She looks towards the hallway as DOCTOR LANE enters, wheeling ELLEN CLAYTON into the room. Doctor Lane is forty, with considerable polish and good looks. ELLEN is in her twenties. She is lovely, fragile and tense. One gets the impression her nerves are at the breaking point. There is a light blanket over her lap.

KAREN. Good afternoon, Doctor Lane.
LANE (*smiling warmly as he wheels Ellen C and stands R of her*) Hello, Karen—(*quickly*)—Mrs Clayton. I was hoping I'd see you before I go.
KAREN (*moving L of Ellen*) I had no intention of letting you leave without saying good-bye. How do you find our patient today?
LANE. I think Ellen's in excellent shape. No reason we shouldn't be able to retire the wheel-chair to the attic in no time.
KAREN. Splendid!

LANE (*to Ellen*) Of course, my girl, you've got to continue with your exercises.

ELLEN (*dully*) I do. I really do them—whenever I remember.

LANE (*sternly*) Ellen, I must impress upon you the importance of helping yourself. There's a limit to what medical science can do. As a matter of fact, *medically* there seems little wrong with you at all.

ELLEN (*quietly*) I know. So you've said . . .

LANE. The treatments, a larger dosage of this invigorating air. That should do the trick.

KAREN. Yes, dear, it really is still warm enough to sit in the sun.

LANE (*indicating the balcony-porch*) And a shame to let that porch overlooking the Channel go to waste.

KAREN. Darling, you used to take such an interest in the garden!

ELLEN (*looking away*) I was interested in many things, Karen.

LANE. You must become interested in them again.

ELLEN. I shall try, Doctor Lane. (*With a faint show of emotion*) I *am* trying. I'm doing my best.

LANE. Yes—yes, certainly you are.

KAREN. Nobody doubts it, my dear. (*Turning to Lane*) You've been so kind, giving us so much of your time.

LANE. My pleasure, Mrs Clayton.

KAREN. We shall miss you.

LANE. I'll only be out of the country a few weeks. It's a most important conference. (*With a smile*) Women go to Paris for the newest fashions. I'm going for lectures on all the latest diseases.

KAREN. John and I had talked of going there again soon. But . . . (*Catching herself up*) Forgive me, Ellen. I shouldn't have brought it up.

ELLEN. Of course you should have! Father was always too busy to take you and then when finally he'd made arrangements, I saw to it that he couldn't!

KAREN (*her hand on Ellen's shoulder, imploringly*) My dear, you've got to stop torturing yourself. (*Continuing as though nothing had disturbed her*) And this young Doctor Phillips who has agreed to look after Ellen has an excellent record.

ELLEN (*with no interest*) Has he?

LANE. I haven't met him but the reports from Whitecliffe are glowing. Luckily his holiday starts tomorrow. He'll stay at Briars and relax. And be on hand for your treatments—or if you need him.

ELLEN. I don't envy him his holiday.

LANE (*trying to control his impatience*) Ellen, Doctor Phillips is doing both of us a great courtesy. I trust we see that he does enjoy his holiday. (*Going to his valise on the coffee-table*) And then, of course, there will be Nurse Pepper.

ELLEN (*sharply*) Nurse Pepper?

LANE (*to Karen, with surprise*) Oh—you hadn't told her?

KAREN. I—I was waiting until you came, Doctor Lane. (*To*

Ellen) You see, the Doctor and I thought it best you have someone again.

ELLEN. A nurse! And you promised no more nurses.

KAREN. My dear, we simply have to have someone. That's all there is to it.

ELLEN. But I thought I was coming along so well!

KAREN. Please, Ellen—don't excite yourself. You *are* much better. And you'll be yourself in no time. But while you still . . .

ELLEN. Another of those harridans hovering over me, fussing, sympathizing! Now I will feel utterly helpless—a burden . . .

KAREN. Darling, that isn't so. You mustn't!

LANE. Yes, try to regard Nurse Pepper as more of a—companion.

ELLEN. I don't want a companion. I don't want someone pouring me hot milk, tucking me into bed and pecking at me with a thermometer! We have Jenny. She takes very good care of me.

KAREN. But Jenny has so much to do. The housework . . .

ELLEN. All my things have been moved downstairs. Father's den has been made into my bedroom. I cause as little fuss as possible. (*She suddenly realizes protest is useless*) Oh—oh, very well. Let her come.

KAREN. Good. I knew you'd be sensible.

ELLEN. We'll see how long she stays. None of the others did. Besides, I thought we'd exhausted the supply of nurses in all of Kent.

LANE. Nurse Pepper is coming from London.

ELLEN. All the way from . . . ? Why on earth is she doing that?

LANE. She doesn't mind a bit of travel. Quite frankly, we thought it advisable to have a stranger. Someone who knew no gossip and wouldn't harp on the past. (*Pleasantly*) Well, since I still have a bit of packing to do . . .

KAREN. Do have a pleasant journey, Doctor Lane. And until two weeks from now, *au revoir*.

LANE. I've left medicine with Jenny. Now remember, Ellen—the treatments, the porch, the garden. There's still so much to enjoy.

KAREN. Of course there is!

ELLEN (*bitterly*) From a wheel-chair? (*Managing a smile*) Good-bye, Doctor Lane.

LANE. Good-bye. And please be considerate of young Doctor Phillips.

ELLEN. I—I'll try.

(DOCTOR LANE *moves* R)

KAREN. I'll see you to your car. (*Indicating the french windows*) Let's go this way. It's quicker.

LANE (*as they go to the french windows*) Thank you. Nothing so flattering as being shown to your car by a lovely woman. Sort of chivalry in reverse.

KAREN. A chivalry I shall continue if I'm to receive compliments.

(LANE *and* KAREN *exit* L.

   ELLEN *sighs wearily, moves her chair over to the coffee-table, takes a cigarette from the box, and lights it. After a few puffs she grinds it out.* JENNY, *cook-housekeeper, enters from the hallway. She is austere, capable. Her face seldom betrays emotion except towards Ellen, of whom she is genuinely fond. She carries newspapers and magazines*)

JENNY. The newspapers from London, Miss Ellen—and your magazines.

ELLEN. Thank you, Jenny. Just put them on the desk.

JENNY (*crossing to the desk, looking towards the porch*) I thought I heard shooting before. They have no right! Poachers!

ELLEN. I hate to hear the shooting. I loathe the thought of things being killed. (*She wheels herself back to* C)

JENNY. We'd all best be keeping our heads indoors! (*Putting the magazines, etc., down on the desk*) Are you warm enough, Miss Ellen?

ELLEN. Yes—I'm warm enough.

JENNY (*moving* L *of Ellen*) Perhaps you'd like me to start the fire?

ELLEN. No—it isn't necessary.

JENNY. You always used to like the fire toward tea-time. You'd come in and lie down in front of it and stare into it . . .

ELLEN. Yes, Jenny, I know.

JENNY. Even when you were a little girl and your father and mother—your *real* mother, that is—would bring you down here on holiday. I'd find you there staring into it and you'd tell me you were seeing princes and princesses and wicked fairies . . .

ELLEN (*impatiently*) Yes, Jenny—yes, I remember!

JENNY. Oh well, you'll be doing all the things you used to—again.

ELLEN. Will I?

JENNY. Now what sort of question is that? A brave, intelligent girl like you won't be long in that contraption. (*Looking at the portrait over the mantel*) You're too much your father's daughter!

ELLEN. Please, Jenny—no inspirational messages. (*Apologetically*) I'm sorry if I sounded cross. But to me the afternoons seem to be getting longer, darker. There's so much more time to think.

JENNY. Then think about getting up and about! Not just sitting there, blaming yourself.

ELLEN. But that's all I can think of! The accident and—(*looking up at the portrait*)—and what I did to him.

JENNY. You've got to stop dwelling in the past. (*Picking up a magazine*) Here—see the new fashions. They should make you laugh. (*She opens the magazine and shakes her head*) Look here, will you now? (*Going to Ellen and showing her*) Going to the theatre, it says. Not much you could see, seated behind that haystack of hair.

ELLEN (*as she looks*) Why, it's Dolly Greer! She's a friend of mine.

JENNY. Dolly Greer . . . Why, isn't she the one who phoned you from London the other day?

ELLEN. Dolly phoned? I didn't know . . .

JENNY. You were having your nap. Didn't your stepmother tell you?

ELLEN. No. I'm sure she didn't.

JENNY. I wrote the message down and gave it to her myself.

ELLEN. It—it must have slipped her mind.

JENNY. Maybe. (*She moves towards the hallway, then pauses*) She was playing the piano before. Your stepmother.

ELLEN. Yes. I thought I heard her.

JENNY. It's been a long time.

ELLEN. *Too* long. I was so glad to hear her.

JENNY. Guess it means she's herself again, that she's over her grieving. If she grieved . . .

ELLEN (*with emotion*) Jenny, don't talk that way! Of course she grieved.

(KAREN *enters* L *with a bunch of flowers*)

(*Hurriedly*) Oh, Karen—I don't recall your telling me that Dolly Greer had phoned.

KAREN (*looking from Jenny to Ellen*) Oh . . . ? Why, I was sure I did. I—I must have forgotten.

(JENNY *stares at her a second, then exits* R)

Darling, I didn't want to upset you. (*Moving to the desk*) She wanted you to come up for the week-end. A dance. I knew you'd never go so . . .

ELLEN. I'd felt rather hurt, not hearing from her. Never hearing from a soul, really.

KAREN. Let's call her back—soon. Perhaps she can come down for a week-end. Yes, whenever you're up to it, dear. (*Snipping the stems of the flowers*) That dress is most becoming, Ellen. You should let me do more shopping for you.

ELLEN. You have enough to do for me, Karen—without choosing my clothes.

KAREN. But I adore buying clothes—even for another woman. I wish you'd wear some of your new things.

ELLEN. Not much point is there?

KAREN. There's nothing so good for the morale! (*She goes to the mantelpiece, takes a vase, empties the old flowers into the fireplace*) I wonder what Nurse Pepper will be like.

ELLEN. Efficient, crisp—with that superior smile reserved for children and lunatics.

KAREN (*taking the vase to the desk and arranging the flowers*) Oh, Lord, I hope not!

ELLEN. A pity she's coming all this way—when she'll be going back so soon.

KAREN. Ellen, please don't be difficult. Doctor Lane thinks it is essential you have someone. You should appreciate his personal interest in your welfare.

ELLEN. His personal interest is in you, Karen.

KAREN. Darling, that's absurd!

ELLEN. He gives it away every time you enter a room. He swallows and chokes like a lovesick undergraduate.

KAREN. Well, dear—at least your imagination is active.

ELLEN (*wheeling herself to the porch door*) I think he's about ready to give up on me anyway. I'm afraid he doesn't believe I want to get well. At times I feel he thinks I'm actually faking.

KAREN. I'm sure nobody realizes more than he, the effort you're making. He understands, too—these things take time.

ELLEN. How much time? It's been five months since the accident.

KAREN (*going to her*) Doctor Lane and I know that you will be well, completely well, as soon as you stop blaming yourself for what happened. (*Earnestly*) It wasn't your fault, Ellen. Nobody thinks it was.

ELLEN. Don't they? I was driving what some of the newspapers called *The Death Car*, wasn't I? Well, I shall never drive again. I'll never step into a car again! (*In a low tone as she looks at the gate on the porch*) Sometimes I'm tempted to wheel myself out on that porch, open that gate and just keep going . . . down . . . down . . . down.

KAREN. Ellen! Don't say anything so horrible! (*Quickly changing the subject*) Let's go out into the garden. I'll have Jenny bring you a sweater, or a scarf. (*She rings the bell by the fire*)

ELLEN. I don't need anything.

KAREN. But you do. It's getting chilly in the afternoons. (*Going to the desk, picking up the vase of flowers*) And today there's a breeze from the Channel. I don't want you catching a cold, my dear.

(JENNY *enters* R)

JENNY. Yes, Mrs Clayton?

KAREN (*going to Jenny with the vase*) Would you put some water in this, please? And bring a scarf for Miss Ellen.

JENNY (*taking the vase*) Yes, Mrs Clayton.

KAREN (*in the doorway, watching after Jenny*) Ellen, I was wondering —does Jenny upset you?

ELLEN. Upset me? Good heavens, no.

KAREN (*moving above the sofa*) She isn't the most cheerful person to have about. I thought perhaps if we found someone else . . .

ELLEN. I feel Jenny is my trusted friend. I wouldn't dream of losing her.

KAREN. Very well, dear. Whatever you say. (*Looking up at the portrait*) I often wonder how John stood her all those years. She did bully him, you know. (*Smilingly*) In spite of the outrageous crush she had on him!

ELLEN. Wasn't it more a case of hero-worship—like so many others?

KAREN. Nothing so mental. Your father was much too attractive. He even looked dashing in court in wig and robe. No—I can't blame Jenny or the others for having a crush on John Clayton.

ELLEN. From all reports when you came into the picture no-one else had a chance.

KAREN (*sitting at the piano*) Indeed they didn't. I saw to that.

ELLEN. It happened so fast. He wrote me he had met you. Only three letters later you were married.

KAREN (*idly playing a gentle tune*) So very fast . . . It's as though fate were guiding your footsteps and suddenly confronted you with a miracle. It was like discovering all those mad, wonderfully delirious emotions you're for ever reading about in books can actually exist—and within yourself. (*As she plays*) The marriage would have happened even sooner if I hadn't been committed for several concerts I couldn't get out of.

ELLEN. You should go back to your career. It's such a waste, staying here, putting up with me. I could manage with just Jenny. Really I could!

KAREN. We'll talk about that when you're well. The world is getting along famously without my Chopin. (*She strikes a chord and rises*) Now you go out and enjoy the last of that sun. I'll bring the scarf out to you. (*She moves to Ellen and starts to help with the chair*)

ELLEN. No, Karen, I can manage.

(ELLEN *wheels herself out* L. KAREN *looks after her, frowning slightly.* JENNY *enters* R, *looking perturbed*)

JENNY. Mrs Clayton.

(KAREN *turns*)

There's a Pepper woman here!

KAREN. So soon . . . ? Very well, Jenny. Please show her in.

JENNY. Mrs Clayton, she's got two suitcases with her!

KAREN. I should expect so. She's stopping here. Miss Pepper is a nurse.

JENNY. Nurse? But Miss Ellen can't stand the sight of those . . .

KAREN (*firmly*) Will you show her in and then please check the linen in her room.

JENNY. That bed's still warm from the last one! (*Defiantly*) Well, as long as she's told right off that nobody puts foot in my kitchen . . . !

(Jenny *exits* R.

Karen *lights a cigarette.* Nurse Pepper *appears in the hallway. She is attractive, warm, with much energy and a friendly smile. She wears a topcoat, hat, carries two suitcases and a handbag. An umbrella dangles from her wrist*)

Karen (*moving* c) How do you do, Nurse Pepper? I am Mrs Clayton. Welcome to Cliff House.

Nurse Pepper. Good afternoon. (*Putting her two suitcases and umbrella down in the hallway*) I'll just leave these here for the present. (*Entering and looking around appreciatively*) Well, now isn't this a lovely place!

Karen. Thank you. You really should have let us know you were arriving today. It's quite a ride from the station in Clifton.

Nurse Pepper (*moving* c) It worked out very nicely, thank you. There was no taxi at the station. And while I was waiting for the bus I just decided to . . . (*Holding up her thumb in a hitch-hike gesture*) Much more economical. And you meet such interesting people!

Karen (*amused*) Really? I'd always thought it rather hazardous.

Nurse Pepper. Nothing ever happens to me. Perhaps because I always take my umbrella. And then, of course, there's always a lady's persuader. (*She draws out her hatpin a bit*) Never have to use it. Guess I'm just not the type to be insulted. (*Remembering*) Oh, but I did send you a telegram that I was arriving today!

Karen. I shall probably get it tomorrow. They phone them from Clifton—when they have a mind to. Anyway, we're delighted you came so soon.

Nurse Pepper. Thank you. Doctor Lane said on the phone I should come as soon as possible. And the case I was engaged on came to a sudden end so . . .

Karen. Oh, I'm sorry. (*She sits in the chair* LC)

Nurse Pepper. Oh, not *that* end. The patient married the doctor. And not a moment too soon. She was running out of illnesses and he was running out of cash. It will be a lovely match.

Karen (*motioning to the sofa*) Please sit down, Nurse.

(Nurse *nods a thank you and sits* c *on the sofa*)

Did you have a pleasant trip?

Nurse Pepper. Just lovely, thank you. There was a dining car. And I do so enjoy eating on trains. Even though it's usually a case of good view and bad digestion. (*Looking around again*) Cliff House! Now there's a splendid name.

Karen. Not very original, I'm afraid. But appropriate. The Channel is two hundred feet below.

Nurse Pepper. Fancy that. Two hundred! Is there a way to get to the beach?

KAREN (*indicating the french windows*) There are some rough steps hewn in the chalk of the Gap. That's about a hundred yards from the house, through the garden there.

NURSE PEPPER (*approvingly*) My—what a perfect hideaway.

KAREN. Hideaway?

NURSE PEPPER (*laughing at herself*) Forgive me. It's those gangster shows I watch on the television. (*She opens her purse and brings out a paper-backed thriller*) And these. I read so many of them I sometimes talk as though I went to school in Chicago. They save my life on night duty. My thrillers and my game of solitaire. Don't know what I'd do without my cards, sitting there waiting for the patient to wake up and complain!

KAREN. In a way you're correct about this place being a hideaway. There are stories that the main structure goes back to the days of smugglers. That it was used to store contraband.

NURSE PEPPER (*greatly impressed*) Of course! Secret rooms and passages. Perhaps even the ghost of a distinguished pirate. Oh, I shall like it here!

KAREN. I hope you will. I presume Doctor Lane told you on the phone about Miss Clayton?

NURSE PEPPER. Yes. He said she baffled the experts—even himself. And when a doctor admits that . . .

KAREN. What else did he tell you?

NURSE PEPPER (*enumerating*) He said her legs are paralyzed. That he strongly feels the condition is psychosomatic. That all we can do is wait for something to make her *want* to get up and walk. Make her want to do desperately she just goes ahead and does it. (*Matter of fact*) And in the meantime keep on feeding her vitamins, from B1 on up.

KAREN. Yes—that about sums it up.

NURSE PEPPER. He also told me she would have a bit of a stroke when she heard about me.

KAREN. She—she was reluctant. But she's resigned to the idea now. (*Rising, to down* L) Did he also tell you how *really* low her morale is?

NURSE PEPPER. Fits of deep depression, tears, anger . . .

KAREN (*moving* C) And what is worse . . . (*In a low tone*) We're worried that in one of her moods she might—well, do something foolish.

NURSE PEPPER. Oh—you mean . . . ?

KAREN. That is why we want someone near her constantly.

NURSE PEPPER. Poor dear. Mrs Clayton, perhaps if you'd give me the details of the accident?

KAREN. It happened on the hill leading from the house. (*She sits* RC) My husband had been ill. Ellen persuaded him to let her take him for a drive. The brake didn't hold for some reason and she was unable to make the horse-shoe turn. Ellen was thrown free.

It was a miracle. But my husband—Mr Clayton—was burned to death.

NURSE PEPPER. What a frightful thing!

KAREN. There was no-one to help. She lay there unconscious while . . . (*She shudders*)

NURSE PEPPER. Couldn't you see the flames from the house?

KAREN. No-one was here unfortunately. I'd gone up to London to the flower show. I hadn't wanted to. But John had insisted.

NURSE PEPPER. And since Miss Ellen was at the wheel she blames herself? But it was an accident. Gracious, they happen all the time.

KAREN. She believes she was crippled as a punishment. It's become a mania. She refuses to step inside a car.

NURSE PEPPER. What about a psychiatrist?

KAREN. She refuses to see one. Fortunately Doctor Lane has a practical knowledge of psychiatry. And he has consulted experts. They agree she must be made to want to walk again. We also should avoid mentioning the accident—even mentioning her father.

NURSE PEPPER. I've known other cases where the patient's been immobilized by shock. Sometimes it takes another shock to make 'em recover. Something equally horrible—or worse.

KAREN. I don't think that's possible. Surely we've had our fill of tragedy here.

NURSE PEPPER. Dreadful, a young girl in such a state. Everything to live for but wanting to die. Well, we'll simply have to see that she changes her plans. I take an interest in a patient, Mrs Clayton. They're always more to me than just a pulse and a temperature and a clean night-gown.

KAREN. I'm glad. I'm also relieved you know about her attitude toward nurses. Jenny will be a bit of a problem, too, I fear.

NURSE PEPPER. Jenny?

KAREN. The cook-housekeeper. Help is difficult to get and we indulge her. In all fairness we haven't been too fortunate in our selection of nurses. The last was all starched efficiency . . .

NURSE PEPPER. I know the type. If you get up in the night for a drink of water by the time you come back, the bed's been made.

KAREN. And then the others. Over-sympathetic, pitying.

NURSE PEPPER. I don't believe in pity, Mrs Clayton. Usually it's a sort of secret satisfaction somebody's worse off than we are.

KAREN (*with a deep sigh*) If you knew how difficult it's all been . . .

NURSE PEPPER (*reassuringly*) Don't worry, my dear. We'll— we'll—(*Rising with spirit as she finds the right word*) we'll *cope?*

KAREN (*rising*) I pray we will. (*Going to the bell*) Now I'm sure you'd like to see your room. I hope you won't find it too dull here after the city. (*She rings*)

NURSE PEPPER. I love sunshine. (*Moving up* C) And tall buildings cast nothing but long shadows.

KAREN. Frankly we were rather surprised at your taking a case so far from London.

NURSE PEPPER. Home is where I hang my cap and shuffle my cards. No ties at all. Why, I could drop into that water below and nobody'd know—except for the ripple.

KAREN. You—you have no family?

NURSE PEPPER. As I told Doctor Lane on the telephone, no-one. Another reason some folks call me the solitaire lady. It's not just my cards.

KAREN. Forgive me. But isn't it rather an eerie feeling, having no-one to know? That is, if anything should happen to you?

NURSE PEPPER. Nothing personal, but belonging to some of the families I've visited would make me feel a lot eerier.

(ELLEN *appears in the french windows. She halts the wheel-chair as she sees Nurse Pepper*)

KAREN (*moving* L) Oh, Ellen, come in. Here is Nurse Pepper.

ELLEN (*wheeling herself* C; *coolly*) How do you do?

NURSE PEPPER. Miss Clayton, I am glad to meet you! (*She extends her hand*)

ELLEN (*ignoring it*) Are you? Why?

NURSE PEPPER (*taken aback; withdrawing her hand*) Oh—oh, I just like meeting people, I expect. I mean, I *am* going to be looking after you and . . .

ELLEN. Are you?

NURSE PEPPER (*cheerfully*) Well, I'm not down here to swim the Channel!

(JENNY *enters* R *carrying the vase of flowers and a thick woollen scarf*)

KAREN. Jenny, you haven't been introduced to Nurse Pepper.

NURSE PEPPER (*very pleasantly; holding out her hand again*) Hello, Jenny—a pleasure.

JENNY (*ignoring the hand as she crosses* L) Hello. (*She puts the vase on the mantelpiece*)

KAREN. As soon as you're settled you might call Doctor Lane. He'll be at Briars until late this afternoon.

(NURSE PEPPER *puts her book back in her bag*)

ELLEN. So you read mysteries, Nurse.

NURSE PEPPER. *Devour's* more the word. And the more blood-letting the more I enjoy them. Oh, I know such things never happen in reality but . . .

ELLEN. Oh? You mean they haven't told you about the murder here at Cliff House? And that *I* was the murderess?

KAREN. Ellen!

NURSE PEPPER (*after a pause; blithely*) Lots of us fancy ourselves as something we're not. When I was your age I just knew I was the answer to Greta Garbo. And look at me today. I'm a sort of Florence Nightingale—with her lamp blown out. (*She moves above the sofa*)

ELLEN. I think you should know we haven't been lucky with our nurses. Not lucky at all. Did they tell you about Mrs Meigs? She was a nurse.

KAREN. Ellen, dear, you're being absurd. (*To Nurse Pepper*) Mrs Meigs was my husband's nurse. She died not long ago. Oh, of natural causes. It was a heart attack. (*Turning to Jenny*) Jenny, will you show Nurse to her room?

(JENNY *goes to Ellen and drapes the scarf over her shoulders.* KAREN *cries out*)

Jenny!

JENNY. What is it?

KAREN. That scarf!

JENNY. What about the scarf?

KAREN. Surely you recognize it. It was Mr Clayton's.

JENNY (*picking up the scarf; with surprise*) Why, so it is. I just reached into the closet and . . .

KAREN. I told you to put all of my husband's things away.

JENNY. I was sure I had, Mrs Clayton. I can't see how I overlooked this.

KAREN (*going to her*) I'm sorry, Ellen, dear. I know how these things upset you.

ELLEN. It's all right, Jenny. (*Tenderly, she reaches for the scarf*) I'll wear it. It's—it's a very warm scarf.

(ELLEN *puts it around her shoulders and* KAREN *wheels her through the french windows.* NURSE PEPPER *looks after them*)

NURSE PEPPER. Yes. She is going to be difficult.

JENNY. Not as difficult as they try to make her! (*Moving* R) I could swear I put that scarf in the attic. (*Abruptly*) Well, are you coming to see your room?

NURSE PEPPER (*gathering up her handbag*) Yes, yes just lead the way.

JENNY (*passing the suitcases*) I don't advise you to put your suitcases away.

(NURSE PEPPER *cheerfully assembles her suitcases and umbrella*)

NURSE PEPPER. Oh, I never do. A suitcase is a wonderful board for a game of solitaire.

(JENNY *exits* R)

(*Following Jenny; her usual jaunty self*) Besides, it saves time later on!

CURTAIN

SCENE 2

SCENE—*The same. Late afternoon, two days later.*

As the CURTAIN *rises,* JENNY *enters* R, *carrying a newspaper and a book. She crosses to the desk, puts the newspaper down, and is about to return the book to the bookcase when shots are heard in the distance. She puts the book on the desk, goes to the porch, and picks up the field-glasses from the table. She then steps out on to the porch and is looking off* L *as* NURSE PEPPER *hurries in* R *and crosses to the telephone. She is wearing uniform and cap.*

NURSE PEPPER (*into the receiver*) Hello—hello . . . Seven-four-three, please. (*She waits impatiently for the connection*) . . . Hello, Doctor Phillips? . . . Well, this is Nurse Pepper at the Clayton place . . . Yes, how do you do? . . . Oh, just fine, thank you. But it isn't me I'm calling about. I wonder if you could come over here at once? . . . Oh, splendid. Splendid.

(JENNY *comes in from the porch to just behind Nurse*)

I know you were told you'd be looking after Miss Clayton, but it's *Mrs* Clayton who doesn't feel well . . . Yes, some sort of fainting spell . . . Oh, I did, and she's come round, but she's very shaky . . . Thank you, sir. Good-bye. (*She hangs up, gives a sigh of relief, turns, and gives a start*) Oh, Jenny—don't ever do that! (*She moves away* L)

JENNY. What's the matter with Mrs Clayton?

NURSE PEPPER. I don't know. We were in her room talking, when suddenly she turned a bit green and fainted.

JENNY. Faint, eh? Never knew her to faint before.

NURSE PEPPER. Well, faint she did! Then I brought her to with a whiff of salts and asked if I should call the doctor. She said no, absolutely no, so I came right down and called him.

JENNY. It had better not be something serious. Enough work here without a new invalid as well as a new nurse to look after. (*She starts to move* R)

NURSE PEPPER. Oh, Jenny, was that you I heard out on the porch last night? *Very* late last night, talking to someone?

JENNY. On the porch? Now what would I be doing out there late at night? I've earned my sleep and I enjoy it.

NURSE PEPPER. There were people there. The shutter was rattling upstairs. I went to close it and heard voices. Mrs Clayton's door was closed so I don't suppose it was she.

JENNY. There's nobody I want to talk to late at night. Sounds indecent.

NURSE PEPPER. It also sounds frightening. (*Going to the porch*) Well, there were voices and from out here. (*Going out on the porch*) Yes, it was whispering. Like conspirators—plotting. (*Looking down over the gate*) My, it's almost a sheer drop into the water!

JENNY (*quietly coming up behind her*) Be careful of that gate, Nurse.

NURSE PEPPER (*trying the gate*) It's locked. (*She realizes Jenny is behind her and backs away quickly*) Tell me, what on earth does it lead down to?

JENNY. It opens on nothing now. The steps go down to a ledge. Mrs Clayton wanted to start some sort of rock garden down there.

NURSE PEPPER. Should think all you could grow would be cliff grass!

JENNY. Not even that. But she bought all sorts of soil, scientific, she called it. Expensive, Mr Clayton called it. Said she was risking her neck, too. Anyway, a heavy storm washed her garden away months ago. Now the steps just stop at that ledge in the middle of the cliff. (*She comes back into the room*)

NURSE PEPPER. My, what a lovely place for a murder. (*Looking down; fascinated*) Steps leading nowhere. Now there's a title, too! (*She comes back into the room*)

JENNY (*scornfully*) Murder. Thrillers! While you're here you should read some of the *good* books Mr Clayton had in his library. None of your trash for him. Steps leading nowhere. Voices in the night, indeed! (*She starts to leave, then stops, turns slowly, and speaks in a low voice*) Unless—unless it was *them*.

NURSE PEPPER. Them! To which particular them are you referring?

JENNY. Those poor souls on the yacht. It was a honeymoon party, headed for the South of France . . .

NURSE PEPPER. Yacht? Honeymoon? Woman, will you be more precise!

JENNY (*slowly, looking toward the gate*) Some say they can be heard any time of night . . . (*Turning to Nurse Pepper*) But, no. No, I don't think Mrs Clayton would want me to tell you.

NURSE PEPPER (*wisely*) Since it's obviously something perfectly ghastly I'd like to see anybody stop you! (*She moves* LC)

JENNY (*going to the porch*) It was ghastly all right, the tragedy. It happened one summer night. The storm came suddenly from the north. The Channel had been like a mirror. All at once there were waves nearly as high as the cliffs. The yacht was tossed and turned like a matchstick, hurtled against the shore like a rubber ball. When it sank everyone was lost. Sometimes when the water is calm you think you see the prow sticking up—(*pointing off*)—there. Right over there toward Abbot's Cliff. And sometimes at night they say you can hear them screaming for help, crying out against the storm.

NURSE PEPPER (*with a sigh*) Yes, I figured it was going to be something on that order. When did this awful thing happen?

JENNY. In nineteen-twenty-seven. The oldsters still talk about it.

NURSE PEPPER. I wonder if they enjoy the telling as much as you.

Anyway, I don't believe it was the unfortunate honeymooners con-
gregating on this porch last night. Not for a second.

JENNY. The late Mrs Meigs used to hear them. Often.

NURSE PEPPER. I don't happen to believe in ghosts the way the
late Mrs Meigs did! And another thing, if you're trying to get me
on the next train to Charing Cross you're wasting your time. I don't
frighten.

JENNY. Oh, I'm not trying to frighten you away, Nurse. Those
things take care of themselves. (*Going to the hallway*) I'll see if Mrs
Clayton wants anything. Fainting . . . And she seemed fit as a fiddle
when I took her her tea a while ago.

NURSE PEPPER (*with interest*) Oh—oh, you took her her tea?

JENNY (*not missing the point*) Of course. Every afternoon. First
Miss Ellen and then Mrs Clayton. Made of herbs and spices. My
own special tea. (*Too politely*) Wouldn't you care for some, Nurse?

NURSE PEPPER (*firmly*) No, thank you. I have an understanding
with my stomach. (*She sighs*) Jenny, can't we try to get along. I
know you don't care for nurses but . . .

JENNY. You're mistaken. I found no fault with Mrs Meigs.

(KAREN *enters* R)

NURSE PEPPER. Mrs Clayton, I asked you to rest.

KAREN. But I don't want to rest. (*Crossing below Jenny to* C) Now
don't look so concerned, Nurse. There's nothing the matter with
me.

NURSE PEPPER. Just a second ago you weren't well at all. (*With a
glance towards Jenny*) You know, after you drank your tea.

KAREN. I feel fine now. In fact since it is cocktail time I think I
shall make some. Jenny, will you bring in ice? You'll join me,
Nurse? A martini *can* be medicinal, you know.

NURSE PEPPER. You're very kind. But I'm afraid the extent of
my indulgence is a passion fruit crush.

JENNY. We haven't any.

(JENNY *exits* R)

NURSE PEPPER. You were right about Jenny, Mrs Clayton. She
certainly isn't overjoyed at having me here.

KAREN. I keep trying to believe her bark is worse than her
intentions. You see, Ellen is determined to keep her on. But sometimes . . .

NURSE PEPPER. No, I don't think we should do anything to dis-
please Miss Ellen.

KAREN (*going to the drinks table*) Oh well, perhaps you will do the
impossible and win her over. (*She prepares her drink*)

NURSE PEPPER. At this point I think it would be easier to steer a
bull by the tail. Mrs Clayton, I wonder if you *should* have a cocktail.

KAREN (*smilingly*) And I wonder if you'd kindly look more like a nurse and less like a female undertaker?

NURSE PEPPER. Some patients find small difference. And I suppose I'd better tell you—I phoned the doctor.

KAREN. Oh, Nurse! (*She moves to the fire*) And he was promised a holiday. Well, I shall simply offer him a drink and send him on his way. (*Realizing*) It will also be an opportunity for him to meet Ellen. Is she still resting?

NURSE PEPPER. As a matter of fact when I went into her room just now I found her attempting to stand. Of course she sat down when she saw me. But isn't that encouraging?

KAREN. Why—why, certainly it is. Most encouraging.

NURSE PEPPER (*hesitantly*) Mrs Clayton, I was wondering. She's such an attractive girl. Isn't there some young man she's interested in, or who's interested in her? That's always such a help in these cases. Matter of fact, in any case.

KAREN. No. No-one. (*Gravely*) There was a young man. It was when she was attending the Sorbonne. She was serious about him. And supposedly he was serious about her. They wanted to marry. Naturally John went to Paris to meet him. But . . .

NURSE PEPPER. Oh, a wrong 'un, eh?

KAREN (*nodding*) Charming. But John had an intuition. As a criminal lawyer he felt he could tell about people. Anyway, he brought her back home.

NURSE PEPPER. Was she very hurt?

KAREN. It was the only thing she and my husband ever quarrelled about. She refused to speak to him for months. And then the boy was involved in some smuggling to-do with Customs. She realized John had saved her from a terrible mistake. (*With concern*) Unfortunately, however, it seems to have turned her against every other young man she has met.

NURSE PEPPER. She'll turn right around when Mr Right comes along!

KAREN. But here . . . We're so remote. There's so little opportunity.

NURSE PEPPER (*with confidence*) It's got nothing to do with geography. Like the rest of nature's conspiracies it just happens.

KAREN. You're very optimistic. I really think it will benefit Ellen, having you around.

(JENNY *enters* R *with a bowl of ice*)

NURSE PEPPER. Thank you, Mrs Clayton. And now I'd better look in on my patient. (*Looking at her watch*) Oh, yes, time for her B twelve. And then I'll see that she pretties up for the young doctor. The postman saw him in the village. He says he's quite handsome.

KAREN. I'm afraid that won't matter to Ellen. Unfortunately.

NURSE PEPPER (*crossing to the hallway*) I'm not so sure. It might be the therapy she's been needing all along.

(NURSE PEPPER *exits* R)

KAREN (*to Jenny*) Nurse is evidently quite a romantic.

JENNY. That's not all. She thinks she heard voices late last night. Out there on the porch.

KAREN. But that's impossible!

JENNY. She seemed quite certain. (*She puts the ice on the drinks table*)

KAREN (*putting ice in her glass*) The only way to get on the porch is through the house. And it was none of us.

JENNY. That's what I tried to tell her. But she said it sounded like two people whispering.

KAREN. It must have been the wind. In these old houses it often sounds deceptively like a voice.

JENNY. Yes, Mrs Clayton. (*She looks at her briefly, then goes to the hallway*) Will that be all, Mrs Clayton?

KAREN. Yes, Jenny. That will be all. And not a word to Ellen about—voices.

(JENNY *exits* R. KAREN *looks towards the porch thoughtfully. Then she turns and notices the book Jenny has put on the desk. She puts down her drink, picks up the book and goes to the bookcase, casually noticing the title. She finds its place on the top shelf and stands on the library stool to replace it.* JENNY *enters* R *and watches Karen, frowning*)

JENNY. Doctor Phillips is here.

KAREN. Ask him to come in, please. (*She steps off the stool and puts the book on one of the lower shelves*)

(JENNY *smiles as she exits.* KAREN *pats at her hair.* COREY PHILLIPS *enters* R. *He is in his mid-twenties, good-looking, casually dressed. He carries a doctor's bag*)

COREY (*moving* C) Mrs Clayton?

KAREN (*meeting him* C) How do you do, Doctor Phillips? I'm sorry you've been inconvenienced. I had a slight fainting spell before and Nurse Pepper became alarmed.

COREY (*smilingly*) You do seem to have made an excellent recovery.

KAREN. I'd been working outside. And the sun was quite warm earlier. Now that you're here will you join me in a cocktail?

COREY. I'd like one very much. However since Nurse Pepper did seem concerned . . . (*He takes her wrist and feels her pulse*)

KAREN. Well, Doctor, shall I live?

COREY. To be a hundred—if your pulse is any indication.

KAREN (*going to the drinks table*) Good. Tell me, how are you enjoying your holiday?

COREY. Briars is a charming cottage. And it's amazing the wonderful time you can have doing absolutely nothing.

KAREN (*mixing a drink*) How fortunate we are all this fits in with your plans. You're on the staff over at Whitecliffe, I believe.

COREY. Yes. I've been there over a year.

KAREN (*going to him with the drink*) I do hope you like martinis.

COREY. My favourite, Mrs Clayton. You're a mind reader. (*Taking the drink*) Thank you.

KAREN (*indicating the sofa*) Doctor Lane explained, of course, about Ellen? (*She sits* LC)

COREY (*sitting* L *on the sofa*) Yes. And left a complete history. I'll admit she sounds a challenge. (*He puts his bag on the coffee-table*)

KAREN (*raising her glass*) Then a toast to your meeting the challenge.

COREY (*raising his glass*) By all means. Doctor Lane said she must be watched carefully.

KAREN. Yes . . . that's why we've engaged Nurse Pepper. Of course Ellen doesn't want a nurse. She doesn't really want a doctor.

COREY. I'm prepared for that, Mrs Clayton. (*Hesitantly*) But there was something that struck me. I wonder if I may speak frankly?

KAREN. Please do.

COREY. Evidently it has occurred to others. I've overheard some gossip from the locals . . .

KAREN. I'm sure you have!

COREY. People seem to wonder if it's wise to keep her out here —where everything must remind her of what happened.

KAREN. I think it's most unwise. I've begged her to let me take her back to London. She refuses to leave. It's almost as though she derived some comfort from being here, where she *is* reminded.

COREY. It could be a part of her condition, punishing herself—seeking retribution.

KAREN. If you knew how we worry! We feel so helpless.

COREY. The accident was several months ago?

(KAREN *nods*)

It does seem a long time for this attitude to persist. However it might disappear as quickly as it came. Most doctors practise a mild psychiatry. I'll see if I can . . .

(ELLEN *and* NURSE PEPPER *enter from the hallway.* ELLEN, *overhearing, smiles cooly as she wheels herself to down* R *of the sofa*)

ELLEN. I don't hold much hope for that.

(NURSE PEPPER *moves above the sofa to* C)

KAREN (*rising*) Oh—Ellen dear, this is Doctor Phillips.

COREY (*rising*) Good afternoon, Miss Clayton.

- ELLEN. Good afternoon.

KAREN. And Nurse Pepper. I'm sure Doctor Lane told you about her.

COREY. He did indeed. A great pleasure, Nurse.

NURSE PEPPER. He told me on the phone about you, too, Doctor. And I'm happy to say he didn't exaggerate a bit. (*Beaming an aside to Karen*) Things are looking up!

COREY (*smiling at Ellen*) Of course you know I'll be giving you your treatments for the next two weeks.

ELLEN. I hope *you* know there are none due until Thursday . . .

KAREN. Doctor Phillips only stopped by to become acquainted, Ellen.

ELLEN (*continuing*) I think you also should know I'm a very bad patient. You see, I don't like the treatments. I don't believe in them.

COREY. Then my first therapy will be to *make* you believe in them.

(ELLEN *stares defiantly at Corey*)

KAREN (*with determined gaiety*) Ellen, dear—a martini?

ELLEN. No, thank you. (*To Corey*) Doctor Lane has failed to make me believe in them.

COREY. How pleasing to my ego if I succeed.

ELLEN. Forgive my lack of optimism, Doctor.

COREY. I have enough for both of us. I think I should warn you I intend to have you out of that chair by the time Doctor Lane returns from France.

ELLEN. In—in two weeks?

(COREY *nods firmly*)

Oh—oh, that's absurd.

KAREN. But wouldn't it be wonderful, dear?

ELLEN. It would be a miracle. Two weeks . . .

NURSE PEPPER. No time limits on miracles, as I recall!

ELLEN (*bitterly*) I suppose you believe in them.

NURSE PEPPER. I believe there's more than just paying our bus fare on the trip through life. I think if we have faith and pray, the miracles will take care of themselves.

ELLEN. And I don't think I'm in the mood for a sermon!

COREY (*putting his glass down on the coffee-table*) Well, I'll be running along I'm glad it was a false alarm, Mrs Clayton. And I'm very glad I've met you, Miss Clayton. (*He picks up his bag*)

KAREN (*crossing below Nurse to L of Corey*) Thank you so much for dropping by. We'll see you on Thursday.

COREY. Thursday, Mrs Clayton. (*Moving above the sofa, L end*) Good-bye, Miss Clayton.

ELLEN. Good-bye—optimist.

(KAREN *moves up* L *of Corey*)

COREY (*easily*) I've been called much worse than that. Good-bye, Nurse. I'm delighted you're on this case.

NURSE PEPPER. Oh—mutual, I'm sure, Doctor.

(COREY *moves* R)

KAREN (*going to the hallway with him*) I'll see you to the door, Doctor Phillips.

COREY. Thank you, Mrs Clayton.

(KAREN *and* COREY *exit* R)

NURSE PEPPER (*looking after him*) My, isn't he the confident young man! I like him.

ELLEN. I don't. That bedside manner, that Harley Street charm . . .

NURSE PEPPER. Well, well—so you noticed his charm.

ELLEN. Professional charm! Looking straight into your eyes! Perhaps he intends to hypnotize me out of this thing.

NURSE PEPPER. As long as he does it, it doesn't matter how.

ELLEN. He thinks I'm some psychopathic freak. I can tell!

NURSE PEPPER (*moving below the sofa*) Shouldn't surprise me if he thought you were an extremely pretty girl with an equally bad disposition. With her pride on her shoulder alongside a chip the size of the cliff.

ELLEN. You—you think I'm a dreadful patient, too. Just as all the rest did. Well, I can't blame you.

NURSE PEPPER. Patients and lovers! They're past understanding. (*Smiling*) You're no more difficult than anyone else. And you'd better not try to be either.

ELLEN (*desperately*) Oh, I wish everyone would go away and leave me alone. That's all I want. To be left alone.

NURSE PEPPER. There's a point of recovery where they all say that. And I say right back, solitude's a good place to visit—but no place to live. (*Going to her*) Nobody can live alone, young lady.

ELLEN (*studying her*) In a way, don't—don't you live alone?

NURSE PEPPER. I'm alone when I push off the light and pull up the eiderdown. And glad of it, at my age.

ELLEN. You—you never married? Never were in love?

NURSE PEPPER. Love! Found out long ago that for me, love's the poisoned apple. And I'm Snow White.

ELLEN. I—I'm sorry. There was something unfortunate . . . ?

NURSE PEPPER (*with a shrug*) You could call it that. He went to sea. Mr Odysseus promised to be back in two years. I sat knitting a pullover and pulling out the threads so I wouldn't make a liar out of him. (*Realistically*) But I'm not lonely. Every case is like a bit of family. And as with most relatives, some you'd choose—the others deserve a nice cup of sedative to quiet 'em permanently.

ELLEN (*almost friendly*) I think I like you. You're not for ever fussing at me like the others. You're—you're *human*.

NURSE PEPPER. Can't take the credit for that.

ELLEN (*firmly*) See that you stay that way.

NURSE PEPPER. I'll stay human all right since I've got little choice. But I'll fuss, young lady, when I've got occasion to! Now that we understand each other, either give me the sack or your right hand.

(*After a slight hesitation* ELLEN *smiles and extends her hand. They shake hands warmly*)

Well, now that we've settled that meeting at the Summit, let's go outside. You haven't been out all day.

ELLEN (*in mock despair*) I might have known. Fussing already!

(KAREN *enters to* R *of Ellen*)

KAREN. That doctor fairly radiates enthusiasm. Oh well, it's natural enough at his age. (*With her arm round Ellen*) However, we mustn't let him raise our hopes too high. We don't want to be—hurt.

ELLEN. You—you don't have to worry about that, Karen. (*Looking towards the french windows*) Now I think I'll go outside. But I want to go alone.

NURSE PEPPER (*picking up the scarf from the side of the wheelchair and putting it over Ellen's shoulders*) I was hoping that we could have a bit of a walk. I haven't seen much of the grounds and . . .

ELLEN. Some other time, Nurse. (*Continuing* L) I'd like to be by myself.

NURSE PEPPER. Very well. But I'll be right in here if you want anything. (*She goes to help with the chair*)

ELLEN. I can manage, Nurse. (*Then she looks up at her and smiles*) But thank you, anyway.

(ELLEN *exits* L)

NURSE PEPPER (*pleased*) You know, I think I've located that chink in the armour already!

KAREN. I'm sure I saw her smile at you. That's progress indeed. (*Going to the fireplace*) And now I must get some fresh flowers for the mantel. (*She takes the flowers from the vase and throws them into the fireplace*)

NURSE PEPPER. You see that they're always fresh, don't you, Mrs Clayton?

KAREN. John loved flowers so! (*Moving down* L) It's the least I can do for him now. You'll keep an eye on Ellen?

Nurse Pepper. Oh, yes, I'll be right here—(*taking a pack of cards from her pocket*)— playing solitaire.

(Karen *exits* L. Nurse Pepper *sits on the sofa, shuffles the cards and starts to lay them out. The telephone rings. She rises, goes to the desk and picks up the receiver*)

Good afternoon, Cliff House . . . Oh, yes, I'll take the message. Just a moment, please. (*She picks up a pencil and writes busily*) Yes, go ahead . . . Yes, will arrive this afternoon on the . . . (*Dropping the pencil in annoyance*) For heaven's sake, I sent that telegram myself yesterday! (*She hangs up*)

(*There is a sudden sound of screaming gulls from the direction of the porch.* Nurse Pepper *turns to look at the porch. As she does so there is the sound of a gun being fired from the garden. A bullet whistles past her and smashes a vase on the table below the opening* R. *She manages to scream, duck, and then shakily stand up. She looks towards the french windows, then at the broken vase, trying to regain her breath.* Karen *enters hurriedly* L)

Karen. Wasn't that a shot?
Nurse Pepper. Indeed it was. Another inch and it would have been a bull's-eye, too.
Karen (*leading her to the sofa*) Are you all right? (*She sits* L *of Nurse*)
Nurse Pepper. Well, my rafters are shaken. But I'm in better condition than that bit of crockery.

(Ellen *wheels herself in, to down* L)

Ellen. Karen, what happened? Nurse Pepper . . . !

(Jenny *runs in* R, *to down* R)

Karen. Somebody fired a shot into this room!
Ellen (*going over to Nurse Pepper*) A shot? But who . . . ?
Jenny. Those poachers! That's who it is. Looking for rabbits.
Nurse Pepper. I can't think of a less likely place to shoot a rabbit!

(Corey *enters* L)

Karen (*with surprise*) Why, Doctor Phillips, I thought you'd gone.
Corey (*moving above the desk to* C) I had trouble starting my car. Didn't I hear a shot?
Karen. There's evidently one of those poachers around. He almost hit Nurse.
Corey (*swiftly crossing above the sofa*) Is there anything I can do?
Nurse Pepper. Do you think . . . ? Well, perhaps just a drop of that medicinal martini . . . ?

KAREN (*going to the drinks table and pouring*) Of course. Oh, I hope this hasn't upset you too much.

JENNY (*levelly*) Yes. A shame if you let it frighten you away.

KAREN (*sharply*) Certainly it won't frighten her away!

ELLEN. Yes, Nurse, you will stay, won't you? I—I'd like you to.

KAREN (*going to down* C *with a drink and also bringing the shaker*) Here, this should help.

COREY. I'm sure you won't let us down.

NURSE PEPPER. Oh, I'll stay if I'm still living. (*She drinks and coughs*) If not, we'll just have to discuss it further!

NURSE PEPPER *takes another sip, rather enjoys it, and is looking at the shaker with interest, as—*

the CURTAIN *falls*

ACT II

Scene i

Scene—*The same. Afternoon, several days later.*

As the Curtain *rises, gulls are heard screaming. It is a grey, brooding day.* Nurse Pepper *is standing on the porch, gazing at the horizon through field-glasses.* Jenny *enters* r *with some letters. She moves noiselessly to the porch, steps out on to it, and stands* r *of Nurse Pepper. After a moment* Nurse Pepper *becomes aware of her.*

Nurse Pepper (*turning*) Jenny, will you stop creeping up on people!

Jenny. See anything interesting?

Nurse Pepper (*moving into the room*) No. Just browsing.

Jenny (*looking off*) It's going to rain. The water looks choppy, too. I wouldn't like to be on it. Dangerous.

Nurse Pepper (*putting the field-glasses down on the drinks table*) I hate to disappoint you but I have no intention of going punting today.

Jenny (*going to the desk with the letters*) I thought perhaps you were looking for the prow of the yacht.

Nurse Pepper. Well, I wasn't. Besides, Mrs Clayton said it had disintegrated years ago.

Jenny. A lot she knows. She's a newcomer in these parts. (*Putting the letters down*) Hear any more voices lately?

Nurse Pepper (*defiantly*) I have come to the definite conclusion it was the wind.

(*Thunder rumbles*)

Jenny. Perhaps it was. That's what they used to tell Mrs Meigs. She knew better. Yes—we're going to have a storm.

Nurse Pepper. From the gleam in your eye I'd say you were expecting nothing less than a hurricane.

Jenny. You don't know our storms, do you, Nurse?

Nurse Pepper. Regardless, I'm staying on come hurricane or light dew! (*Good-naturedly*) Jenny. I'm sure your favourite book is *Rebecca* and your favourite heroine is Mrs Danvers.

(Ellen *wheels herself on from* r *to* c. *She seems brighter, and wears a gaily coloured dress*)

Ellen. Jenny, have you seen Mrs Clayton?

JENNY. She went upstairs a while ago, Miss Ellen. (*Moving* R)
Said she had to work on the accounts.

ELLEN. Thank you. There's something I wanted to ask her. But
it can wait.

(*There is another rumble of thunder*)

JENNY. I was just telling Nurse about our storms. The terrible
destruction they often cause; the gales from the North Sea.

(JENNY *exits*)

NURSE PEPPER. Whenever that woman's around me she carries
on like a grounded witch.

ELLEN. She was so loyal to my father we overlook her disposition.

NURSE PEPPER (*noticing*) My, don't we look pretty this afternoon!
You should have called me to help you, Miss Ellen.

ELLEN. I wanted to see if I could manage by myself. Well, I did.
(*Too casually*) And, besides, such a gloomy day. I thought something
colourful . . .

NURSE PEPPER. Oh, I'm sure. And also the doctor's stopping by.
As if you needed to be reminded.

ELLEN. Oh, is he? I'd quite forgot.

NURSE PEPPER. A likely story. New dress, an hour combing your
hair. (*Shaking her head*) I can't believe it's for me and those gulls out
there.

ELLEN. I—I tell you I simply felt like dressing up a bit. (*Giving
in*) Oh, all right. I admit Doctor Phillips has made me feel better
in six days than Doctor Lane has in six months.

NURSE PEPPER. Of course it's his medical skill. It couldn't be his
looks or his youth.

ELLEN (*soberly*) It's his assurance. It seems so—so genuine. As
though he really is determined to have me walking again.

NURSE PEPPER. But has he you believing it, too? That's the
important thing.

ELLEN. Sometimes I almost dare. Oh, if you knew how I wanted
to! I don't know how long it will take but Corey makes it seem so
possible.

NURSE PEPPER. Corey, eh? Already on a first name basis. That's
a good sign in a patient-doctor relationship.

ELLEN. He thought perhaps if we were less formal. You understand?

NURSE PEPPER. I began to understand when I saw you two in the
garden yesterday. Throwing in some free calls, isn't he?

ELLEN. I didn't know you saw.

NURSE PEPPER (*delicately*) I withdrew discreetly.

ELLEN. He was just driving by and—well, he's getting rather
lonely down at Briars. (*Eagerly*) You—you like him, Nurse?

NURSE PEPPER. As a doctor he's doing very well. As a man—well, evidently from the look in your eye he's downright smashing.

(KAREN *enters* R *with a sheaf of bills and a cheque-book*)

KAREN. Oh? Am I interrupting a private conversation?

NURSE PEPPER (*moving up stage*) Just girl talk, Mrs Clayton.

ELLEN. I was telling Nurse that suddenly it doesn't seem so hopeless, my being able to walk again.

KAREN (*crossing above Ellen*) Darling, Doctor Lane has been telling you that for months. Won't he be pleased to find you in such good spirits! (*Going to the desk*) In the meantime you must try to co-operate with that young Doctor Phillips.

NURSE PEPPER. Oh, she's trying.

KAREN (*smilingly*) Oh, I see what you mean. (*She sits behind the desk*) That's the first time you've worn that dress, Ellen. (*Picking up letters*) Very encouraging.

ELLEN. Karen, I was thinking—I'd like to have some friends down for the week-end. Perhaps next week. Just a few.

KAREN. You would? Why—why, certainly, dear. If you're sure you're up to it.

ELLEN. I haven't seen any of my friends. I'd like to now. I can't stay in hiding for ever.

NURSE PEPPER. Good girl. You're coming along nicely.

KAREN. We'll talk about it next week, Ellen.

ELLEN. I could write them notes today.

KAREN. Darling, would that be wise? Let's call them on the phone next week. Perhaps you'll change your mind and won't feel up to it. It would be most awkward if . . .

ELLEN. But, Karen, I'm sure I shall!

KAREN. Ellen, a few of your friends came down before and you refused to see them. I had to turn them away. You tormented yourself for weeks. This way you'll have no regrets if you change your mind.

ELLEN (*in a low voice*) I—I suppose you're right.

KAREN. My dear, it's only to spare you embarrassment.

(NURSE PEPPER *disapproves of the decision but remains quiet*)

NURSE PEPPER (*consulting her watch*) Yes—time for vitamin B fourteen! I'll get our pills, Miss Ellen.

(NURSE PEPPER *exits* R)

KAREN (*opening an envelope containing a bank statement and cancelled cheques*) The miracle that young doctor promised hasn't happened just yet, my dear. Why, what . . . ? (*In dismay*) Dear, I'm sorry! I've opened your bank statement by mistake.

ELLEN. It makes no difference.

KAREN. But this cancelled cheque! It's none of my affair but this cheque made out to Jenny, Ellen, it's for two hundred pounds.

ELLEN. Oh, that. I didn't tell you about it. I was afraid you wouldn't approve.

KAREN. I don't. Jenny is paid extremely well. I think she's overpaid.

ELLEN. It isn't for her. It's for the missionary charity at her church. They hadn't met their quota. It's for a good cause.

KAREN. She had no right to ask you for money. I shall speak to her.

ELLEN. Don't, Karen. After all, the money isn't doing me much good. I'm glad I could help.

KAREN. Very well. After all, it *is* your money. I simply don't want you taken advantage of.

ELLEN. I trust Jenny, Karen.

KAREN (*picking up the bills and rising to make room for Ellen*) While we're discussing money, here are the household bills for the past month. I've made out the cheques. They need your signature.

ELLEN (*wheeling herself to behind the desk*) Thank you. (*Busying herself with the cheques*) I don't know how I'd manage without you. I'm so stupid about these things.

KAREN (*moving L of Ellen*) It's no effort on my part, dear. Naturally I wish I could contribute more to the household. But until I go back to my concerts . . .

ELLEN. You contribute more than enough. I'll never be able to repay you. (*Picking up a pen, indicating the bills*) I hate this time of month.

KAREN. That, my darling, is a universal emotion.

ELLEN. You know what I mean. Why should *I* be doing this? It should be your money. I never could understand about the will.

KAREN. Your father simply never got around to making out a new one. After all, he was comparatively young. Many men are careless about such things. They put them off.

ELLEN. But you should let me give you . . .

KAREN (*interrupting*) Let's not go over this again. Your offer is most generous but I have enough money to manage comfortably. I've never been greedy about money.

ELLEN. But Father loved you so!

KAREN. And I loved him. It didn't matter whether he left me a million pounds or a brass farthing. Please believe me, Ellen. It was your father who was my life . . .

(ELLEN *looks up at her.* NURSE PEPPER *enters* R *with pills and a tumbler of water.* ELLEN *turns away and buries her face in her hands*)

ELLEN. Oh, Karen, I wish I'd been killed, too! How I wish it!

KAREN (*quickly*) Why, Ellen—you mustn't!

NURSE PEPPER (*moving L*) What is it, Miss Ellen!

KAREN. I'm afraid it's my fault. We were discussing her father and . . .

NURSE PEPPER (*going to* R *of Ellen*) And just a second ago you were so gay. Now you stop that, young lady. The doctor will be here any minute, and you don't want him to see you all red eyes and sniffles!

ELLEN (*dabbing at her eyes*) I'm sorry, I thought I could control myself. I'll—I'll be all right. (*Reaching for Karen's hand*) It wasn't your fault, Karen. Forgive me—for making a scene.

KAREN. All forgotten. Perhaps we'd better forget these cheques, too, for the time being.

ELLEN. They've got to be signed. I'll do them.

KAREN (*picking up a letter*) Oh, Nurse—here's a letter for you.

NURSE PEPPER. Indeed? (*She takes the letter from Karen, smiling broadly at Ellen in an effort to cheer her*) Now who could be writing to me? I pay cash for everything. (*Examining the letter*) Oh, my land-lady. (*She puts the letter down on the desk, takes a pill from the bottle*) Better take our pill, young lady! It's overdue.

ELLEN (*dispiritedly*) Which one is this?

NURSE PEPPER. The very latest! So new they haven't invented what it's good for.

KAREN (*crossing above to the hallway*) Let me know when Doctor Phillips is through with you, Ellen. It would be pleasant if we all had a drink together.

(KAREN *exits* R.

NURSE *watches as* ELLEN *takes her pill and sips her water.* ELLEN *next resumes signing cheques.* NURSE *sits on the sofa, takes a paper-back from her pocket and commences to read.* ELLEN *quietly dabs her eyes again.* NURSE *looks at her*)

NURSE PEPPER. And you think you have troubles, Miss Ellen. Now take the girl in this book. They're just found her in the refrigerator. Anyway, slices of her are found there. Wrapped in aluminium foil. (*Considering*) Well, at least the killer was tidy.

ELLEN (*smiling*) Thanks for trying to cheer me up.

NURSE PEPPER (*returning to her book*) Nothing like these fairy-tales for us people nothing ever happens to.

ELLEN. You're forgetting you were almost shot the other day.

NURSE PEPPER. There was nothing personal about that bullet. But whoever took the meat chopper to this young lady knew every detail of her anatomy intimately.

(ELLEN *laughs*)

That's more like it. Now stay that way until the doctor comes.

ELLEN. I try to get a grip on myself. But then things remind me and I think back . . .

NURSE PEPPER. No point in thinking back! The past is what we forget to learn from, the present is a mess of our doing so the future's our only hope. (*Kindly*) And, besides, getting that nice new dress all tear-stained!

ELLEN. You probably thought I was silly, dressing up. Wanting to give a party.

NURSE PEPPER. I thought it most normal. And don't you fret. You'll have your week-end party.

ELLEN. I do feel ready to see people again. And I'd so enjoy planning it! I wish Karen hadn't been so doubtful.

NURSE PEPPER (*without much conviction*) Oh—oh, she meant it for your own good.

(NURSE *returns to her book as* ELLEN *resumes work. She reads with increasing interest. Unable to resist, she turns to the end of the book. She reads with surprise, shakes her head sceptically*)

Imagine a clever murderer falling for a trick like that! (*Booming out, in threatening tones*) You can't get away with it! The place is surrounded!

(ELLEN *looks at* NURSE *as she shrugs, and puts the book back in her pocket.* JENNY *enters* R)

JENNY. Doctor Phillips is here. (*She crosses to* L)

(COREY *enters* R, *with his bag*)

COREY. Good afternoon. Hello, Nurse. (*He moves above the sofa*)

JENNY (*going to the desk*) May I borrow the newspaper for a while, Miss Ellen?

ELLEN. Yes, Jenny—certainly.

(JENNY *picks up the newspaper, spies Nurse's letter and, unseen, picks it up, too.* JENNY *exits* R)

COREY (*crossing to* R *of Ellen*) Young lady, have you been crying? (*Concerned, putting his bag down on the desk*) Ellen, what is it? What's happened?

ELLEN. Nothing. Everything. I'm such an utter fool. I think I've improved and then . . .

COREY. Do you know what happened, Nurse?

NURSE PEPPER (*rising to* C) Well, she's been simply fine all day. I wasn't here but it seems she and Mrs Clayton were discussing her father and . . .

COREY. I wish Mrs Clayton would choose other topics to talk about!

ELLEN (*quickly*) She's not to blame. It's that I can't help feeling so awful, sitting here signing these cheques. I have no right.

COREY. Ellen, I—I don't understand.

NURSE PEPPER. Especially if you have the money to cover them.

ELLEN. That's just it. I've got practically everything. For some reason father neglected to make a new will when he married Karen.

COREY. That's hardly your fault.

ELLEN. But he loved her so. I've begged her to let me make it up to her. But she says her happiness with him was more than enough. She won't take a penny.

COREY (*moving up stage*) Mrs Clayton doesn't appear in exactly dire straits.

ELLEN. She's not. But it's so unfair. (*Slowly, as she wheels herself below Corey to* C) Of course I've arranged that if anything should happen to me . . .

COREY (*moving to* L *of Ellen; drily*) If I'm reading your mind correctly, isn't the sacrifice you're thinking of a bit excessive?

ELLEN (*after a pause; quickly*) Oh, I didn't mean *that*. Really I didn't.

COREY. I thought my job was to make you want to walk. I didn't know I'd also have to make you want to live.

ELLEN (*steadily*) A few weeks ago I might have meant that the way it sounded. But you must believe me, I feel so different now. If anyone has given me hope—it's you.

NURSE PEPPER. That's true, Doctor Phillips. She 'old me so. Even put on her pretty dress for you.

(ELLEN *gives her a look*)

Now never you mind! The poor boy deserves *some* encouragement.

COREY. I'm flattered. And it's a delightful frock. (*Forcefully*) Now you've got to believe *me*, things are going to be all right. As long as we know you want them to be. You owe it to yourself and to Mrs Clayton—and to me.

NURSE PEPPER. And to me.

ELLEN (*with a laugh*) Then obviously I have no choice.

COREY. Absolutely none.

(NURSE PEPPER *looks towards the french windows and gasps*)

NURSE PEPPER. Look!

COREY. What is it?

NURSE PEPPER. There—there was someone looking in through the windows!

(COREY *goes over to the french windows, opens them, and takes a few steps outside*)

Be—be careful!

COREY (*reappearing*) There's no-one there, Nurse. Are you sure you . . . ?

NURSE PEPPER. I did! It was a man in a trench-coat. (*She hurries over and looks out*) That's odd. There's nobody . . . (*With a shrug*) Oh well, as long as it wasn't another poacher lining up his target!

COREY. If there *was* someone I'm sure he merely mistook the path. (*To Ellen*) Now I think we'd best get busy with the exercises. I want you out of that chair by the time Doctor Lane returns. (*Wheeling Ellen towards the hallway*) I'll call you, Nurse—if we need you.

NURSE PEPPER (*still looking into the garden*) Oh, you won't be needing me.

(COREY *and* ELLEN *exit* R. NURSE PEPPER *stands mystified, then sighs, goes to the sofa and absent-mindedly takes her pack of cards from her pocket. She sits on the sofa and shuffles the cards, occasionally looking at the french windows. Suddenly she recalls, saying aloud*)

Of course, my letter. (*She rises, goes to the desk and searches for her letter, lifting the doctor's bag*)

(JENNY *enters* R *with a bowl of flowers*)

JENNY (*crossing to the fire*) Hope this pleases her ladyship. I snipped 'em too short the last time.

NURSE PEPPER. Amazing. Simply amazing!

JENNY (*putting the flowers on the mantelpiece*) What's so amazing about a bunch of flowers?

NURSE PEPPER (*looking on the floor behind the deck*) I am not referring to the flowers. They're one of *God's* little mysteries.

JENNY. What is it now?

NURSE PEPPER. My letter. You know, my letter from my land-lady.

JENNY. I don't know anything about your letter from your land-lady.

NURSE PEPPER (*rising*) I got a letter and put it down to give Miss Ellen her pill and then when I went to pick it up it was gone.

JENNY (*slowly*) My, lots of strange things happen to you in this house, don't they? Almost as though it were warning you . . .

NURSE PEPPER. Jenny, if you're playing games with my mail I'll have you know it's a criminal offence!

JENNY. Cliff House didn't like the other nurses either. It seemed to be driving them away so *she'd* be forced to take Miss Ellen back to London . . . where she belongs.

NURSE PEPPER (*moving to below the sofa*) I thought Miss Ellen was the one who wanted to stay here!

JENNY. You believe everything you're told, don't you, Nurse?

NURSE PEPPER (*lifting the sofa cushions, then stops*) Oh, what am I doing? I didn't have it over here.

JENNY (*taking the letter from her pocket and slipping it on to the desk*) It will turn up. If there *was* a letter. (*Moving to* C) That new doctor seems to have perked Miss Ellen up. Always said she needed something to take her mind off what happened. Instead of forcing it down her throat.

NURSE PEPPER (*still concentrating on the letter*) What are you talking about now? (*She sits on the sofa, feeling in her pockets*)

JENNY. Take the portrait over the fireplace. Used to hang in the hall. After the accident the new Mrs Clayton had it brought here. Said that's where Miss Ellen wanted it. *There.* Where he'd be looking her straight in the eyes all the time. (*She moves* R) Making her think of that night. Not likely!

NURSE PEPPER (*stopping her search for the letter*) Jenny, the—the night of the accident. Where were you?

JENNY (*moving* R *of the sofa*) Over in Clifton. There was a church social.

NURSE PEPPER. And Mrs Clayton was in London?

JENNY. So she says.

NURSE PEPPER (*very casually*) Just how new is the new Mrs Clayton? I mean, how long were she and Mr Clayton married?

JENNY. About a year. Why?

NURSE PEPPER. Oh—oh, just curious. He was very methodical, wasn't he? I mean, he'd been a good lawyer?

JENNY. He was a fine lawyer! One of the best.

NURSE PEPPER (*shuffling her cards*) Then that makes it doubly odd . . .

JENNY. What's odd?

NURSE PEPPER. The fact he never made out a new will.

JENNY (*flustered and then angry*) Oh, that. Well, maybe he had his reasons. Besides, why should she get her hands on all that money? She was only married to him a little while. So, it belongs to Miss Ellen!

NURSE PEPPER. But she was his wife. They were very happy, I'm told. Well, weren't they?

JENNY (*with a shrug, moving up* C) You should have heard the argument about having a garden on that stretch of ledge down below. He said it was nonsense, that she was off her rocker. But she went ahead with it anyway.

(KAREN *appears in the hallway*)

They had other quarrels, too. But the one about the ledge was the worst. Seems only right the storm came and swept the garden away.

KAREN (*moving up* C) That will do, Jenny.

(JENNY *turns in surprise, then starts towards the hallway*)

I don't want to hear you gossiping about me again?

JENNY (*unmoved*) Very well, Mrs Clayton.

(JENNY *exits* R)

NURSE PEPPER (*putting her cards away in her pocket*) I—I must admit I did ask her a few things.

KAREN. I'm surprised you had to ask. (*Going to the desk*) Mr Clayton and I did quarrel about the garden below. And I dare say he was right, considering what happened to it.

NURSE PEPPER (*rising*) Well, it's a very novel retreat—(*going to the porch*)—but those steps leading down to it. I never could keep my balance. Vertigo, that's my trouble. (*Stepping out on to the porch*) They have to lead me to the Underground.

(*Gulls above suddenly commence to scream*)

(*Looking up*) Wonder what bit of jetsam has set them off. (*She looks down, grasps the rail, weakly manages to scream, and backs away*) Mrs— Mrs Clayton!

KAREN. Nurse, what is it? (*She moves up* C)

NURSE PEPPER (*backing into the doorway*) There's—there's something down there.

KAREN. Down—down on the ledge?

NURSE PEPPER. No, below. Below on the beach!

KAREN. For heaven's sake, what is it?

NURSE PEPPER (*turning to face her, trying to sound calm*) Now—now don't be alarmed, dear. But I do believe it's a body.

KAREN. A body? Oh well, it—it would be someone in bathing. A few do quite late, you know.

(*The gulls are quiet.* KAREN *hurries to the table, picks up the field-glasses, goes out on to the porch*)

Where did you think you saw it?

(NURSE PEPPER *follows her and gingerly peers over*)

NURSE PEPPER. Straight down below. (*Looking about*) Well, it was there a minute ago.

KAREN (*focusing the glasses, searching*) I don't see anything. No— there's nothing there now. Nurse, you almost frightened me to death. If there was anything it must have been driftwood—or, as I said, a bather.

NURSE PEPPER. Then it was driftwood or a bather in a top-coat! And it was floating stretched out like a corpse! (*She takes the glasses and looks frantically*) Maybe the tide's taken it out—or in—or something.

(COREY *enters* R)

COREY. Oh, good afternoon, Mrs Clayton. I forgot my bag.

NURSE PEPPER (*still looking*) There *was*—I know there was . . .

(COREY *looks questioningly at Nurse Pepper*)

KAREN. We've just had a bit of excitement. (*Returning into the room*) Nurse thought she saw a body on the beach below.

COREY (*amused*) Indeed? Anyone we know?

KAREN. I saw nothing. Perhaps if you look . . . ?

COREY. Glad to oblige. Nothing makes my day so complete as spotting a corpse in the surf. (*Going to the porch*) Nurse, perhaps it was the man you saw peering in the window.

KAREN. Man in the window?

COREY (*going out on to the porch*) Yes, a while ago. Nurse said she saw someone. *I* didn't.

NURSE PEPPER (*handing him the glasses*) That man was wearing a trench-coat! The floating object was in a top-coat. And he hadn't worn it in for a swim, either!

(COREY *looks over*)

(*Searching with him*) Well?

COREY (*straightening up and shaking his head*) Nurse, what did you have for lunch?

NURSE PEPPER. I did see someone! At least, it was something dressed like someone.

(COREY *moves back into the room*)

Now don't tell me I'm beginning to see men this late in life! Especially men who aren't there.

COREY (*to Karen; knowingly*) Spinsters, you know . . .

(KAREN *nods sympathetically*)

NURSE PEPPER (*turning to them suddenly*) And the gulls! What about the gulls? Their racket?

COREY (*listening carefully to the silent air*) What gulls?

NURSE PEPPER (*defeated*) Oh—oh, it's a conspiracy. That's what it is!

(COREY *puts the glasses on the drinks table*)

KAREN. Quite often things do float in. But so far, never a body.

(COREY *goes to the desk to get his bag*)

How is the patient, Doctor?

COREY. I think in better spirits now. Evidently she'd been wrought up about something.

KAREN. Yes, I'm sorry about that.

COREY. Those scenes have got to be avoided, Mrs Clayton. If we want her to recover.

KAREN. I try to be so careful. But sometimes . . .

(COREY *goes to the hallway*)

When you're finished with Ellen, let's all have a drink.

COREY. I'd like that very much.

(COREY *exits* R)

NURSE PEPPER (*coming in from the porch*) Well—could have been driftwood. But a belt and coat-tails? (*Going to Karen*) And there's something else. My letter! Mrs Clayton, my letter from London. I put it down for a second and next I knew it was gone.

KAREN. That hardly seems possible. Where did you put the letter down?

NURSE PEPPER. On the desk.

KAREN (*picking up the letter*) Is this the letter?

NURSE PEPPER (*going to her*) Why, yes—so it is! Where do you suppose it came from?

KAREN. I think you said London.

NURSE PEPPER (*disturbed*) Oh, that's not what I meant! I mean just now. (*Thoughtfully*) It's all very, very peculiar.

KAREN. I hardly think anyone is playing hide and seek with your mail. (*Not unkindly*) Perhaps it *was* something you had for lunch. Or maybe you've been working too hard.

NURSE PEPPER. I'm not overworked. (*Opening the envelope*) And I had an omelette for lunch. Of course, Jenny prepared it . . . (*She cries out*) Mrs Clayton, it's empty!

KAREN (*understandingly*) That sounds like something I'd do. Seal and mail the envelope without the letter.

NURSE PEPPER (*angrily*) Sounds like a policy of harassment to me. The letter wasn't on the desk and then after everyone's been in here and gone, it reappears. Only it's just an empty envelope! (*She moves up* C)

KAREN. Proving only you have an absent-minded correspondent. (*Going to the hallway*) A body down below, a face in the window, a vanishing letter. Really, Nurse . . .

NURSE PEPPER. Very well, just to prove to myself that I wasn't seeing things, how did you say one gets to the beach?

KAREN (*with a nod towards the french windows*) Only by using the hewn steps in the Gap. But it would be dangerous, not knowing the way.

NURSE PEPPER (*moving to the french windows and looking off*) I don't care about the danger. I'm going down and see for myself. Why, possibly something could still be done for him.

KAREN. It's very steep and winding. Besides, it's getting dark. (*With finality*) I suggest you wait until morning. Then if you still care to, I'll go with you.

NURS PEPPER. I tell you, I'm not afraid.

KAREN (*very softly*) That is a great mistake.

(KAREN *exits* R)

NURSE PEPPER (*hesitates, then murmurs aloud*) In the morning, indeed! I'll get my coat and go now.

NURSE PEPPER *starts to move* R. *As she does so, another peal of thunder is heard, and the bookcase* R *of the fireplace slowly swings open.* NURSE PEPPER *hears the faint noise, stops short and listens. The bookcase is quickly closed.* NURSE PEPPER *plucks up courage to turn, sees nothing, and shakes her head in relief. She hurries out* R. *Thunder again, as the sky darkens.* NURSE PEPPER *returns, throwing on her coat. She crosses* L *and hurries out through the french windows. After a moment the bookcase opens again and* DOCTOR LANE *emerges from inside, wearing a trench-coat and a hat. He goes swiftly to the french windows and stands there, lighting a cigarette as his eyes follow Nurse Pepper. He pulls down the brim of his hat and noiselessly exits after her. Thunder is heard again as—*

the CURTAIN *falls*

SCENE 2

SCENE—*The same. Half-past eight the same night.*

When the CURTAIN *rises* KAREN *is playing the piano. The piece is Liszt's second Hungarian Rhapsody, and she is near the conclusion. Her playing is loud and turbulent, as though she were trying to blot out everything but the music. The curtains at the balcony porch are parted, and the night outside is clear.* ELLEN *wheels herself in from the hallway* R, *and comes* C. KAREN *finishes the Rhapsody, pauses, then looks over at Ellen.*

ELLEN (*in a strained voice*) That—that was beautiful, Karen.

KAREN. Well, at any rate—a release.

ELLEN. Are they still down below?

KAREN. I don't know. (*Rising, going out on to the porch and looking down over the gate*) I believe they've finished. I see no light. (*Looking up at the sky*) The storm has blown over. The Sky is clear. There's even a moon.

ELLEN (*shuddering*) Such a terrible thing to have happen. It's so ugly and so sad. The poor man. Who do you suppose he was?

KAREN. He surely will carry some identification. (*Moving* R *of her*) Darling, do try not to think about it.

ELLEN. I can't help thinking about him. Wondering who he is and how he ever ended up down there.

KAREN. Perhaps you should go to your room. They'll be back up soon. You don't want to hear the morbid details.

ELLEN. I'd like to stay and see Corey.

KAREN. Corey? Oh, yes, Doctor Phillips. Seems odd somehow, calling a doctor by his first name.

ELLEN. I—I really feel he's more of a friend.

KAREN. Don't tell me it's another case of a patient becoming infatuated with her handsome young doctor?

ELLEN. No, Karen—it's not that.

KAREN. Good. I think it's just as well. All things considered.

ELLEN. You don't have to worry. I've considered everything. You—you do like him?

KAREN. Very much. It's merely that I'm thinking of you. There's no reason to be hurt again unnecessarily. You remember the other time, Ellen.

ELLEN. I can't very well forget.

KAREN. Darling, you do realize your father was correct? I know it never makes it any easier at the time. But . . .

ELLEN. He didn't really know him! But, please, let's not talk about it. Anyway, about Doctor Phillips—I know I have no right to think about anybody until I'm out of this chair.

KAREN (gently) At least I'm happy to know you're no longer so embittered. (After a pause; with sudden enthusiasm) Ellen, I've the most wonderful idea! Since you are feeling so much better, how about a holiday, a change? Just you and me.

ELLEN. Go away? But . . .

KAREN. It will do us both a world of good. Oh, we should have done it long ago.

ELLEN. But, Karen, I really don't . . . Where did you want to go?

KAREN. Oh—some place really exciting, gay. South of France, Italy. (Her hand on Ellen's shoulder) That's where your father and I spent our honeymoon. I should so love to see it again—with you. (Moving away R) And you know, my dear, I actually think I might begin to play again—really start work—if I got away.

ELLEN. Oh, I want you to, Karen. I wish you would. But surely I'd be a burden!

KAREN. Burden? Nonsense! Besides, I'm sure you'll be walking again soon. Darling, surely you know I wouldn't go and leave you.

ELLEN. But Nurse is here. And Corey feels he's making such progress!

KAREN (after a pause, firmly) Ellen, I believe a change is imperative for both of us.

ELLEN. When—when did you want to go?

KAREN. There's nothing to keep us. I could make arrangements in a day or two.

ELLEN. And how long would we stay?

KAREN. Oh—a month or so. If all goes well, even longer.

ELLEN. And, of course, when we return Corey would be gone. (She wheels herself to the fireplace and stares into it)

KAREN (moving to R of her) Ellen, you can see Doctor Phillips whenever you want to!

ELLEN (*dully*) Can I, Karen? *Should* I? (*Still looking into the fireplace*) I know why you're suggesting this trip. Very well, I'll go. What difference does it make.

KAREN. In the long run you won't be sorry, my dear.

ELLEN (*moving below Karen to* c) But at the moment the long run never matters a dam.

(NURSE PEPPER *enters* R)

NURSE PEPPER. Well, they're taking the poor soul away. My, such an unpleasant fate. Gives me the shivers to think of it.

KAREN. Are they all going?

NURSE PEPPER (*moving* R *of Ellen*) The sergeant, the constable and two ambulance men are still in the kitchen. Jenny's giving them hot tea and sandwiches and a piece of her mind about wet boots. Oh, and Doctor Phillips is there, too. Poor boy, he had to examine the body.

KAREN (*moving* L *of Ellen*) Did they find out who the man was?

NURSE PEPPER. There was nothing to identify him. Not even a wallet. He'd been in the water several days. Must have fallen in somehow and drowned.

KAREN. Horrible, having such a thing happen here.

NURSE PEPPER. It didn't have to happen here. There's a lot of water out there.

KAREN. Oh, I see. Of course it could have drifted here.

NURSE PEPPER. Could have. But not from too far. The constable says it's been a slow current for a week. (*With a look at Karen*) So I guess it wasn't the omelette I had for lunch after all.

KAREN. I'm sorry I doubted you. But I couldn't see anything. Neither could Doctor Phillips.

NURSE PEPPER. Well, it was too late to be of any help to the poor chap anyway.

KAREN. But letting you go down there alone!

NURSE PEPPER (*after a pause; lightly*) Oh—I wasn't alone.

ELLEN. What do you mean?

NURSE PEPPER. I mean there was somebody behind me all the way.

KAREN. I don't understand.

NURSE PEPPER. I was followed. I've got a sense about such things. After years of sitting up nights in hospital corridors and outside bedroom doors, my hearing's acute, too.

KAREN. Surely you're mistaken! Who could it have been?

NURSE PEPPER. Perhaps the man I thought was peeping in through those windows. When I turned there was nobody. I decided I'd better keep going. He might have been embarrassed if I'd turned round and bumped into him.

KAREN. Couldn't it have been an animal? Of course, a stray dog!

NURSE PEPPER (*taking a handkerchief from her pocket*) Mrs Clayton. I'd like to meet the dog—(*unrolling the handkerchief*)—who smokes these. (*She holds a half-smoked cigarette*) Naturally I didn't loiter when I saw the body. I found this on the way back up. Imported—and expensive.

KAREN. But—but it could have been there for days!

NURSE PEPPER. Not still burning, it couldn't.

KAREN. Did you tell the constable?

NURSE PEPPER. He was not impressed. The sergeant said some women think they're always being followed. Then he suggested it was *my* cigarette. When I told him I didn't smoke he said sometimes couples come out this way to—well, to talk. That I might have interrupted their—conversation. And frightened them away.

KAREN. I warned you of danger. I told you not to go down there!

NURSE PEPPER (*with a shrug, rolling the cigarette up in the handkerchief*) I had to find out if I was right. Besides, there are times in any profession when a girl has to toss her bonnet over the windmill. (*Confidentially, returning the cigarette to her pocket*) Not that there weren't moments today when I wished I'd gone in for needlework instead.

ELLEN (*shivering*) I'd have been frightened to death.

KAREN (*moving to the porch door*) Darling, you should go to your room, rest awhile. (*She draws the curtains*)

ELLEN. I couldn't rest. I never felt more wide awake.

(COREY *enters* R)

COREY. Well, here's hoping that's the end of a grim bit of work.

KAREN (*moving above Ellen and Nurse to* L *of Corey*) Poor Doctor Phillips, it must have been an ordeal. Can I get you anything?

COREY. No, thank you. The tea just hit the spot.

KAREN. Then perhaps the others. Are they still here?

COREY. Jenny is just about to hand them their hats.

KAREN. I'll go speak to them. (*Crossing Corey to the hallway*) Oh, Ellen—why not tell the doctor our thrilling news?

ELLEN. News?

KAREN. Why, yes, dear. About our holiday.

(KAREN *exits* R)

COREY. Holiday? What does she mean?

ELLEN. Karen wants me to go away with her.

COREY. When?

ELLEN. In a day or so.

COREY (*crossing below Nurse to Ellen*) This seems rather sudden. Why is she taking you away now?

ELLEN. She thinks a change would do us good. I suppose she's right.

COREY. But she can't take you away! Not when we're so close to . . . Ellen, do you want to go?

ELLEN (*looking away*) Karen seems very anxious to.

NURSE PEPPER (*starting for the hallway*) I think if you'll excuse me . . .

COREY. Nurse, please stay! I think you're on my side. And I shall need your support.

(NURSE PEPPER *halts*)

Ellen, I don't care what Mrs Clayton wanted. How about you?

ELLEN (*wavering*) I—I told her I'd rather stay here. Nurse Pepper could look after me. But Karen says she doesn't want to leave me.

COREY. I'm afraid she'll have to. You can't go now. Not when I feel you're almost well. (*Turning to Nurse Pepper*) Doesn't it seem highly irregular to you?

NURSE PEPPER (*helplessly*) Well, it's not general procedure to move away the patient when he's responding to treatment. And she's responding.

ELLEN (*unhappily*) I'm sure Karen has her reasons.

COREY. So am I. However I have reasons for wanting you to stay. Perhaps I have no right to rant this way but I'm not just a doctor talking to his patient. Ellen, there's so much more involved.

ELLEN. Corey, there—there mustn't be.

NURSE PEPPER (*starting for the hallway again*) Poor Jenny, someone should really help her with that floor.

COREY. No, Nurse—please.

(NURSE PEPPER *pauses*)

I want you to know that what I feel for Ellen isn't merely a professional interest.

NURSE PEPPER. That's nice. But why don't you tell *her?*

COREY. I'm certain that she knows. You do, don't you, Ellen?

ELLEN. But, Corey, it's so wrong. So hopeless! The sensible thing would be to stop seeing each other.

COREY. How could it be, if you feel the same about me?

ELLEN (*smiling tenderly*) You know I do. From the first day I met you. You were so arrogant, so—so downright smug. I loved you right off.

COREY. It happened that way with me, too. I thought you were rude, mean-tempered, spoiled. I also knew I was your slave.

NURSE PEPPER (*again starting for the hallway*) Well, I'll leave you two to your compliments and . . .

ELLEN. *Please*, Nurse.

(NURSE PEPPER *dutifully halts again*)

It's my turn to need your support. I've got to make him see. It's got to stop right here. The best thing is for me to go with Karen.

COREY. That's the damndest logic I ever heard. Since we love each other, why?

ELLEN. Because it's not fair to you. Me, like this. (*She slaps the side of the chair in futility*)

COREY. It wouldn't be fair if you went away. (*Kneeling beside her, looking into her eyes*) Ellen, it's been decided for you. You're going to stay with us and get well.

ELLEN (*studying his face; brokenly*) If—if you really think it will happen soon. If you're willing to wait and work with me. And have the most enormous patience.

COREY. There's no patience more enormous. But it won't take any time at all. Just trust me.

ELLEN. Then I shan't go with Karen. You see, she didn't understand how you felt. She was trying to spare me.

COREY. Perhaps . . .

NURSE PEPPER (*beaming*) Now that's all settled I'm *sure* you'll want to be alone.

COREY. I've got a better idea. I think Ellen and I should go some place and celebrate. Make our plans. (*Rising*) There's a full moon tonight. We could go for a drive and enjoy it.

ELLEN (*hesitantly*) Drive? Oh, I don't think so. I haven't been in a car since . . .

COREY. I know. And it's high time you were. You're surely not afraid with me?

ELLEN. It's myself I'm afraid of! Of the way I might act!

COREY. Let me worry about that. You've got to get used to cars again, young lady. Might as well start tonight.

ELLEN. I'll try, Corey. I've got to stop being such a coward. (*Reaching for his hand*) And as long as I'm with you . . .

COREY. Then let's go. We'd be fools to waste such a night. Don't you agree, Nurse?

NURSE PEPPER. I always agree when the doctor prescribes. Now shall I get your coat?

ELLEN. It's just in the hall. Corey will get it for me.

COREY (*wheeling her below Nurse Pepper towards the hallway*) We'll see you later, Nurse.

ELLEN. Do you realize it's the first time I've been away from the house in five months!

COREY (*with a laugh*) Then let's make it a real occasion. All the way to Folkestone and back!

(COREY and ELLEN *exit* R.

NURSE PEPPER *smiles approvingly. Then she looks off through the french windows as she thinks of the cigarette. She takes the handkerchief from her pocket and unwraps the cigarette. She studies it, goes to the ashtray on the coffee-table and examines the contents. She finds no similar brand. She goes to the ashtray on the desk, is searching among the butts as* JENNY *enters* R)

JENNY (*after watching her a moment*) No need to be doing that.

(*Taking a package of cigarettes from her pocket and moving* c) Have one of mine.

NURSE PEPPER (*startled*) Jenny! (*Recovering her poise*) I—I was just looking for something. (*She moves below the sofa*)

JENNY (*going towards the bookcase*) So am I. Something to look at in bed tonight.

NURSE PEPPER (*sitting on the sofa*) Help yourself. There's bound to be a lovely tragedy, taking place around a kitchen sink or in a graveyard. (*She takes the pack of cards from her pocket*)

JENNY. Mr Clayton's library contains only the best. His books were like his friends. All carefully chosen. But you wouldn't understand.

NURSE PEPPER (*shuffling the cards; half-aloud*) Suppose I should be terribly rude if I told her to go beat her tambourine.

JENNY (*going to the bookcase*) They are my friends, too. And like friends they will hold your secrets . . . even be trusted to keep them. (*She takes from the lower shelf the book Karen placed there in Act One, Scene Two. She pats it and smiles enigmatically*) But sometimes the best place to hide a secret is in the open. (*She replaces the book in the same place*)

NURSE PEPPER. Wha . . . ? (*She turns and looks at her in puzzlement*) And sometimes all cuckoos aren't found in clocks!

JENNY (*looking up at the painting of John Clayton*) My secret will always be safe. I did the right thing. I know.

NURSE PEPPER (*impatiently, trying to concentrate on the cards*) Isn't this your night to go prowl the heath, Lady Macbeth?

JENNY (*locates a large leather-bound book and tucks it under her arm*) That man they brought up from below. I wonder when the next will be found.

NURSE PEPPER. The next what?

JENNY. Body, of course. (*She moves up* c)

NURSE PEPPER. Aren't you being unduly pessimistic?

JENNY (*opening the porch curtains*) Those things always happen in threes. Haven't you noticed? Perhaps he's been there a long, long time. Since the disaster.

NURSE PEPPER. Thought you said that was back in nineteen-twenty-seven.

JENNY. It was.

NURSE PEPPER. Then allow me to inform you that scientifically, medically and biologically that is an utter impossibility.

JENNY (*moving down* c) Science! An awful lot of things science can't explain.

NURSE PEPPER (*giving her a look; patience exhausted*) You can say that again, my girl.

JENNY. There are many still unaccounted for. If he was one of them at least now he can rest. But those others still wandering—still coming up from the sea . . .

Nurse Pepper. Really, Jenny—every night to you is All Hallows' Eve!

(Karen *enters* r)

Karen. They've gone, Jenny. You can tidy up now.
Jenny. Very well, Mrs Clayton. (*Referring to the book she is carrying*) Miss Ellen won't mind. I want to see some pictures.
Karen. Very well. Take it along.

(Jenny *exits* r)

I saw Ellen's chair in the hall. (*Moving* c) What does it mean?
Nurse Pepper. It means she and Doctor Phillips went for a ride.
Karen (*with surprise*) A ride? In a car?
Nurse Pepper. Exactly. There's a full moon, you see.
Karen (*crossing to the french windows*) When did they leave?
Nurse Pepper. Only a few moments ago.
Karen. She swore she'd never set foot in a car again. How did he ever persuade her?
Nurse Pepper. Didn't need much persuasion. That young chap has a way with him.
Karen. So it seems. (*Troubled*) I wish she'd consulted me. The least little thing might set her back.
Nurse Pepper (*with feeling*) If you ask me a bit of relaxation will do her good.
Karen (*smiling pleasantly*) Yes, I suppose you're right. Poor dear, it's time she enjoyed herself. (*Going to the desk*) It's been such a hectic day I think I shall go to my room. (*She opens the drawer and takes out a torch, unobserved by Nurse Pepper*) If you'd like to retire, Nurse—I'm sure we'll hear them when they return. (*She moves down* c)
Nurse Pepper. Thank you, Mrs Clayton. But I'll wait up.
Karen (*yawning*) My, I *am* tired. Good night, Nurse.
Nurse Pepper (*smiling*) Good . . . (*In dismay, as she notices Karen's shoes*) Why, your shoes! Those pretty shoes.
Karen (*looking down at them*) What about them?
Nurse Pepper. You've got mud on them.
Karen. So I have. (*Crossing below the sofa to the hallway*) The constable and the others must have tracked it into the kitchen. Oh well, it will brush right off. Good night again.
Nurse Pepper. Good night.

(Karen *exits* r. Nurse Pepper *resumes her game of solitaire. Suddenly she becomes uneasy. She looks over her shoulder, then towards the french windows. She rises, crosses and locks them. Then she returns and resumes her game. She is yielding to temptation—and is about to hurry it along when the lights go out. The stage is illuminated by only the faint light from outside*)

(*With irritation*) Jenny, I'll give you one second to put those lights back on! (*Crossly*) Well. Jenny—the second is up. (*She turns, looks for Jenny in the dark, speaks with less certainty*) Jenny—Jenny, that *is* you?

(NURSE PEPPER *rises, goes to light switch* R *and clicks it to no avail. She crosses to the fire to light the candles when suddenly from the balcony porch comes a strange, baffling sound. It is the noise of someone climbing up the steps on the side of the cliff. She gasps*)

NURSE PEPPER. On the steps—it isn't possible . . .

(*Terrified,* NURSE PEPPER *draws back into the shadows between the downstage bookcase and the french windows, pressing tightly against the wall. A man can be seen as he comes on to the porch. He wears an oilskin coat that glistens in the moonlight. His hat is pulled down over his forehead. He opens the gate. It creaks ominously, making a grating sound as it swings.* NURSE PEPPER *is unable to control a moan as he steps on to the porch. Quietly, swiftly he crosses to the right bookcase, opens it and steps inside. He pulls it shut after him. The gate still swings in the wind.* NURSE PEPPER *steps out of the shadows, looks towards the bookcase in bewilderment. Then she manages a scream as she runs towards the hallway.* KAREN *appears in the hallway with the lighted torch*)

KAREN. Was that you, Nurse?
NURSE PEPPER (*trying to get her breath*) Yes—yes, it certainly was.
KAREN. What happened to the lights? What happened to you?
NURSE PEPPER (*with difficulty*) Oh, Mrs Clayton—even if I could talk you'd never believe what I was saying. (*Haltingly*) There—there was a man. (*Pointing to the porch*) He came up from there. He came up—the steps!
KAREN. You're hysterical. It isn't possible!
NURSE PEPPER. You've got to believe me! A man, straight up from the water.
KAREN (*crossing below her to the fire*) You must have fallen asleep and had a nightmare. (*Lighting the candles*) Those steps lead down to the ledge. The water's many feet below.
NURSE PEPPER. I don't care how he did it. The frightening thing is that he did! (*Pointing to the gate*) There! Look at that gate swinging!
KAREN. It could have come ajar in the wind. But, very well, if a man came up those steps where is he now?
NURSE PEPPER. Oh dear, you'll never believe this either! He walked into the bookcase.
KAREN. Walked into . . . ! No, I certainly don't believe it. (*Ringing the bell*) Perhaps Jenny can tell us what happened to the lights.
NURSE PEPPER (*going to her*) Mrs Clayton, I know it sounds incredible but a man disappeared into your bookcase!
KAREN (*moving to the desk*) Very well, we shall see.
NURSE PEPPER. What—what are you going to do?
KAREN (*taking a pistol from a drawer*) See this. In case he decides

to walk *out* of the bookcase. (*Starting towards the bookcase*) Now just to prove it was a dream . . .

Nurse Pepper. Let's not prove anything. Let's just get out of here. We're only human. He's supernatural!

Karen. We'll see if there's some way to swing this open. (*Handing her the pistol*) Here, hold this, please.

Nurse Pepper (*taking the pistol very gingerly*) What—what am I supposed to do with this thing?

Karen (*exploring the woodwork around the bookcase*) I suggest if your friend reappears you pull the trigger. We'll see how supernatural he is. (*Pounding softly*) It doesn't seem to be hollow. No, I'm sure you're mistaken.

(Corey *enters* r *with a torch*)

Corey. Mrs Clayton, what happened?

(Nurse Pepper *wheels around, with gun pointed*)

(*Moving* c) Nurse, be careful!

(Ellen *wheels herself in* r)

Karen. Nurse thinks she saw someone come up those outside steps. Then she says he vanished into the bookcase.

Corey. Into the bookcase?

Nurse Pepper. Yes, he did. And it wasn't the kidney stew I had for supper!

Ellen. What happened to the lights? I looked back and saw them go out. All over the house.

Karen. I don't know. I rang for Jenny. I can't imagine what's keeping her. I give up. I can find no way to make the bookcase budge. (*She moves away up* lc)

Nurse Pepper. There has to be an opening! He couldn't just walk through—or maybe in this house he could. It's that Jenny who's at the back of all this. Trying to scare me back to London. Well, she's got to think of something worse than this!

Corey (*turning* r) I'll see about the lights. (*He stops*) Why— what's this? (*He bends, picks up an object and examines it with his flashlight*)

Ellen. What is it?

Corey (*hoarsely*) It's—it's a piece of seaweed!

Nurse Pepper. Seaweed? My, she went to a lot of bother, didn't she?

Karen. Seaweed! Then there must have been someone who came in here.

Nurse Pepper. I told you a man did. (*Hurrying over to the bookcase*) There's a way to get this thing open and I intend to find it!

(Nurse Pepper *puts the pistol down on the mantelpiece and works feverishly on the panelling. There is a click, then the noise of the section slowly opening.* NURSE PEPPER *draws back*)

There, I told you.

(JENNY *is seen standing in the opening*)

Jenny, really—this is going too far!

(JENNY *takes a few faltering steps, then suddenly falls to the floor in front of* NURSE PEPPER, *who screams*)

ELLEN (*clinging to Corey*) Corey, is—is she dead?

NURSE PEPPER (*kneeling and bending over Jenny*) Perhaps she's only fainted. (*Feeling Jenny's pulse*) She's still alive, but I don't like the look of her.

COREY. Quick, some brandy.

(NURSE PEPPER *lifts Jenny's head into her lap.* KAREN *goes to the drinks table and pours brandy.* COREY *moves* R *of Jenny.* JENNY *faintly mumbles something into Nurse Pepper's ear*)

NURSE PEPPER. Yes, Jenny? What are you trying to say?

(JENNY *mutters again*)

What? I can't quite . . .

KAREN (*moving above Jenny with the brandy; sharply*) What is she saying?

(JENNY *falls back*)

NURSE PEPPER. Jenny!

(COREY *feels Jenny's pulse, then uses his torch to see her better*)

COREY. She's—she's dead.

KAREN. Dead! But she hadn't been ill!

COREY (*standing up; grimly*) She didn't have to be. There's blood coming out from just below her heart. She's been stabbed.

KAREN. Stabbed? (*Moving above the desk*) Then we've got to call the police at once!

(NURSE PEPPER *rises and fetches a cushion from the sofa*)

COREY. Perhaps we should get out of here. We don't know who or what is roaming about.

(NURSE PEPPER *puts the cushion under Jenny's head*)

KAREN. The police must be notified. *Murder* . . .

(KAREN *is interrupted by a sudden loud noise from the driveway. It is like the sound of a giant firecracker exploding*)

Nurse Pepper. My goodness, what was that?

(*A red glow starts to illuminate the candle-lit room. It increases and flickers violently as they look towards the french windows.* Corey *rushes over* L)

Corey. It's—it's the car! It's ablaze.

(Karen *and* Nurse Pepper *join Corey at the french windows.* Ellen *wheels herself across* L)

Karen. Whose car?
Corey (*opening the windows*) My car, Mrs Clayton. That explosion came from my car. (*He turns and faces her, frowning*)
Nurse Pepper. And just a minute ago you and Ellen were in it!

They are all watching the flames in the distance, as—

the Curtain *falls*

ACT III

SCENE—*The same. One o'clock the following afternoon.*

As the CURTAIN *rises, gulls are heard. It is another grey day and shadows have already entered the room.* KAREN *is standing at the french windows, looking out.* NURSE PEPPER *enters* R, *carrying several bed-sheets. She crosses to the desk and puts them on it.*

NURSE PEPPER (*as she crosses*) Have the police gone, Mrs Clayton?
KAREN. Yes, that's the last of them—for a while. (*Turning*) How is Miss Ellen?
NURSE PEPPER. We're doing very well. And out suitcase is packed. She said she wanted to be alone for a bit. (*Picking up a sheet*) I'm sure that once we get the poor dear away from here . . .
KAREN. Thank heaven they gave us permission to stay at the inn. Not only for Ellen's sake. For *all* our sakes.
NURSE PEPPER. Oh, I agree. (*Flouncing out the sheet*) I find myself starting at so many shadows I feel like a ballet dancer.
KAREN (*going to the desk*) Of course we've got to be available whenever they want us.
NURSE PEPPER (*with relish*) And then the inquest! (*Taking the sheet to the chair* LC) I do enjoy them on the screen. And here I am, a featured player in the flesh.
KAREN. Why would anyone kill Jenny? Her whole life seemed to be Cliff House. *Us.* The church in the village.

(NURSE PEPPER *covers the chair with the sheet*)

Had you noticed anything strange about her last night?
NURSE PEPPER. Poor soul, she was no stranger than usual. Around me she always acted like a candidate for immortality in the Chamber of Horrors.
KAREN. Just before she died—I got the impression she said something to you.
NURSE PEPPER (*very busily tucking in the sheet*) Oh, did you?
KAREN. Did she, Nurse?
NURSE PEPPER. Well, there was sort of a—a moan. Really only natural under the circumstances.
KAREN. I thought perhaps she'd recognized who stabbed her. That she was trying to tell us. (*She picks up a sheet*)
NURSE PEPPER. Oh, if only she had! Now don't you bother with the furniture. You'd best go finish your packing. I can manage in here.
KAREN. That's awfully kind of you. (*With feeling, glancing around*)

I don't think I shall ever set foot in this place again. And once I was so happy here. (*She moves above the sofa with the sheet*)

NURSE PEPPER. You'll be much better off at the inn. (*Moving up* C *to* L *of Karen*) Not that you haven't weathered it beautifully. The murder, the police, those reporters . . . (*Tight-lipped*) Oh, those reporters. Motive, indeed! I think of all the women in the world Jenny was the least likely to be cavorting with a married man. (*Taking the sheet from Karen*) Having Doctor Phillips at her side was indeed a great comfort to Miss Ellen.

KAREN. Yes—it seems to have been a help.

NURSE PEPPER. You do like him, Mrs Clayton?

KAREN. He's evidently a charming young man.

(*The bookcase starts to swing slowly open*)

Nurse!

NURSE PEPPER (*dropping the sheet*) What now?

(KAREN *points in horror to the bookcase*)

(*Mildly*) Oh, that. I thought for a moment you'd seen a mouse. (*Realizing, and doing a "take"*) Oh, no—not again!

(COREY *enters through the bookcase, leaving the section ajar*)

COREY. Oh, sorry. I didn't mean to frighten you.

NURSE PEPPER (*taking a deep breath*) Quite all right. We're getting used to it by now.

COREY. That's a very ingenious contraption. This opening leads to the cellar and the cellar has a passage-way that connects with the ledge on the cliff. You never noticed anything down there, Mrs Claton?

KAREN. Of course I noticed a tiny cave. But I never investigated where it lead to. It was too dank, unpleasant.

COREY (*moving to* L *of Nurse Pepper*) And you never knew this bookcase led down to the cellar?

KAREN (*coolly*) I've never been in the cellar.

NURSE PEPPER. This place really must have been a smugglers' paradise!

KAREN. But how could they have got to and from the ledge from the water?

NURSE PEPPER. I doubt if they sat and waited for a high tide. (*Suddenly*) Of course! A rope ladder. Raised and lowered on signal. Yes, that should have done it very nicely.

COREY. You very possibly have something there, Nurse.

KAREN. But last night—the man she saw coming up the steps from below. How did he get *to* the ledge.

NURSE PEPPER. How do we know he wasn't in the house all the time? He could have gone down from the cellar. Then when he came back he used the outside.

COREY (*with a glance towards the porch*) He even could have gone down from the outside. He wouldn't have been seen. As I recall, those curtains were drawn.

KAREN. *I* closed them, Doctor. Ellen was nervous. But why was he doing all this manœuvring?

NURSE PEPPER. Not for the exercise! Perhaps he wanted to scare me to death—or scare me out of here.

COREY. You're positive it was a man? The lights were out.

NURSE PEPPER. There was moonlight. It was a man.

COREY. You did tell the police that Jenny enjoyed frightening you.

NURSE PEPPER. Not to the extent of putting on a raincoat, going down to that ledge, climbing back up again, opening the bookcase and stabbing herself! No, not even Jenny.

COREY. Oh, I don't think she stabbed herself.

NURSE PEPPER (*crossing below Corey to the desk and picking up the ashtray*) Neither do the police. (*She sifts the cigarette butts*)

KAREN. Well, I must start getting ready. There's no need to do that. There's been nobody here but the police and the reporters. (*She moves* R)

NURSE PEPPER (*emptying the ashtray into the fireplace*) Oh, I trust the police.

KAREN (*pausing in the hallway*) Oh, thank you again, Doctor—for convincing them it was essential that we leave.

COREY. Ellen couldn't possibly stay here. I'm amazed at her control, as it is.

(KAREN *exits* R. COREY *looks at Nurse Pepper and hesitates*)

Nurse . . .

NURSE PEPPER (*replacing the ashtray on the desk*) Yes?

COREY. Just before she died I—well, it seemed to me that Jenny whispered something to you.

NURSE PEPPER (*moving above the sofa*) My—fancy that.

COREY. Well, did she?

NURSE PEPPER (*picking up the sheet*) There *was* a sort of gasp.

COREY. That's all? Just a gasp?

NURSE PEPPER (*draping the sheet over the sofa*) Now you couldn't expect her to pass the time of day in her condition. (*She moves below the sofa, arranging the sheet*)

COREY. I think she was trying to tell you something. Poor woman, if only she could have managed it. (*Glancing at his watch*) I've got some errands. Miss Ellen said I could use her car. (*He moves above the sofa*)

NURSE PEPPER. A shame about yours, Doctor. But how lucky you weren't in it!

COREY (*grimly*) A great disappointment to somebody. To be

precise, the person who introduced a kerosene-soaked cloth to my gas tank.

NURSE PEPPER. Oh, Doctor, there's something else that's been troubling me—that bit of seaweed you picked up last night. Might I see it?

COREY. Just as I told the police, for the life of me I can't think where I put it.

NURSE PEPPER (*moving by* L *of the sofa to up* C) I think I saw you put it in your pocket.

COREY. Oh? Perhaps I did. (*He feels in pockets and brings out a small green leaf*) Here it is.

NURSE PEPPER (*moving to him and examining it*) A leaf! It could have been blown from anywhere. Yes—I didn't think the stranger brought it up from the sea.

COREY. But last night it was wet and looked like seaweed.

NURSE PEPPER. It probably just got stuck to his shoe. Don't you think?

COREY (*with a weary smile*) I think we'd better leave the sleuthing to the experts. All we can get is more confused. (*Moving* R) I'll look in on Ellen. (*Suddenly*) Oh, yes, there's another thing. I know that Mrs Clayton and Jenny didn't get along. Did they have a quarrel last night?

NURSE PEPPER. No—no, not that I know of.

COREY. You see, when I asked if it could have been a woman who came up from the ledge I didn't mean Jenny.

(COREY *exits* R)

NURSE PEPPER. But . . . Oh, no, not Mrs Clayton. (*She thinks back and shakes her head*) Goes into the bookcase—then comes right in from the hallway. No, there'd have to be two of her! (*She goes to the sofa. Busily concentrating on the events, she absent-mindedly commences to make the sofa up as a bed. She is smoothing the sheet, expertly executing hospital corners before she realizes what she is doing. She sighs at herself, pulls it undone and throws the sheet loosely over the sofa. She sees the ashtray on the coffee-table, looks at the butts carefully, then crosses to the fireplace and throws them into it. The bookcase, still ajar, catches her attention. She peers inside timidly. She takes a step inside, then quickly retreats and slams it shut. She breathes a sigh of relief, gets a sheet from the desk and starts to unfold it*)

(LANE *enters through the french windows*)

LANE (*immediately behind her*) I beg your pardon.

NURSE PEPPER (*turning around rapidly*) Where—where did *you* come from?

LANE. From the driveway. I'm sorry if I startled you.

NURSE PEPPER. Oh, think nothing of it. I'm startled so often here I get nervous when I'm not. (*Suspiciously*) Now you're not another of those reporter chaps?

LANE. No, Nurse, nothing so romantic. I'm Doctor Lane.

NURSE PEPPER. Doctor Lane! Well, fancy that. It's high time that we met. Oh, not that I feel we're strangers.

LANE (*genially*) Oh, we're not strangers. Not at all. I just got back about an hour ago. I heard what had happened here and naturally came straight out.

NURSE PEPPER (*moving* C) I'll go tell Mrs Clayton you're here.

LANE (*following to* LC) I'm afraid I involved you in a rather unusual case.

NURSE PEPPER. It certainly hasn't been dull. But here I am, safe and sound at the finish. And the patient's doing very nicely.

LANE. That is good news. You see, Miss Clayton was the only patient I felt guilty about leaving.

NURSE PEPPER (*moving above the sofa to* R) No need for that. She got better as soon as you left! Oh dear, what I mean is Doctor Phillips seems to be just what the doctor ordered. I really think somehow or other he's going to get that girl on her feet again. (*Emphatically*) And such a relief in Cliff House, a hand reaching out for a hand—instead of a throat.

(NURSE PEPPER *exits* R)

LANE (*waits, then cautiously looks towards the phone; he goes to it, picks it up and speaks in a low voice*) Hello, nine-four-two, please . . . Hello, Lane speaking . . . Has he arrived? . . . Well, when he does tell him I shall be a few minutes late . . . Yes, as soon as I can. (*He hangs up, takes a cigarette from his case and lights it from the lighter on the desk. He then moves to the french windows*)

(KAREN *enters* R)

KAREN (*moving above the sofa to* C) Doctor Lane! This is a pleasant surprise.

LANE (*meeting Karen* C) Mrs Clayton, how good to see you again. (*He takes her hand*)

KAREN. We didn't expect you for two or three days.

LANE. I got through earlier than I expected.

KAREN (*with a wave toward the covered furniture, moving below the sofa*) You must forgive the eerie appearance.

LANE (*moving down* L *of her*) I was so sorry to hear about what happened. Ghastly business.

KAREN (*in a low voice*) We can talk. (*She sits* R *on the sofa*) They're busy inside. He's still here, too.

LANE (*sitting* L *of her*) How do you feel?

KAREN. I don't let myself know. No sleep, the police all last night and this morning. How much more of this can I take?

LANE (*urgently*) Karen, we've got to force their hand. We haven't much time.

KAREN. I was afraid of that.

LANE. You mustn't be afraid now. Not when we're this close.

KAREN. I—I suppose you're right. We're moving into the inn. He got us permission.

LANE. Convenient . . .

KAREN. It's all so cruel, so heartless. (*Rising*) It doesn't seem . . .

LANE (*rising*) You have the gun?

KAREN (*going to the desk*) Why, yes. I gave it to Nurse Pepper last night. In the excitement I'm not sure I put it back. (*She opens the drawer and takes out the pistol*) Yes, here it is.

LANE (*moving to R of the desk*) Let me see if it's loaded. (*He puts his cigarette in the ashtray and checks the gun*) No—it's empty!

KAREN. That's impossible! It was loaded. I know it was! Somebody must have . . .

LANE. Never mind now. You've got more bullets?

KAREN (*reaching back into the drawer*) Yes—farther back in here. (*Taking out a package*) Here they are.

LANE (*taking the bullets and quickly reloading the gun*) You might need this.

KAREN (*with a sigh*) I know how to use it. (*Nervously*) How much do you think they know?

LANE (*moving round the LC chair to above the desk*) They certainly must be convinced someone else was here last night. Unless Nurse Pepper was having an hallucination. (*He hands her the gun*) Put this where you can get it readily.

KAREN (*returning the gun to the drawer*) This is as good a place as any. (*She wavers, leans against the desk*)

LANE. Steady now. In just a few hours . . .

KAREN. I'm so afraid something will go wrong. That one little slip which usually occurs. At least in fiction.

LANE. There's going to be no slip. (*He picks up his cigarette and puffs*)

(NURSE PEPPER *and* COREY *enter* R. COREY *is carrying Ellen's suitcases*)

NURSE PEPPER. Doctor Lane, here's Doctor Phillips. He was so surprised to hear you were back.

COREY (*putting the luggage down*) But terribly pleased, sir. (*He goes to him and extends his hand*) An honour to meet you.

LANE (*as they shake hands*) I've had excellent reports. I can't thank you enough.

COREY. I've enjoyed it. How was France?

LANE. The conference was most successful. But I'm afraid your holiday hasn't been what I promised.

COREY. It was—up until last night. (*With a smile*) And there have been many compensations. I dare say you'll be wanting your cottage so I'll be getting my things out.

LANE. Not at all, Phillips. Stay on at Briars until your vacation is over.

COREY. Thank you, sir. I'll take you up on that. (*He picks up one suitcase and crosses below Lane to the french windows*) I'll put Ellen's things in the car.

(NURSE PEPPER *picks up the second case and follows Corey*)

I'll be back in a jiffy, Mrs Clayton—to drive her to the inn.

KAREN (*quickly*) But there's no need. I shall have plenty of room in my car.

COREY. She asked me to drive her in. And I'm sure you'll need help with your luggage.

KAREN. You're—you're very kind.

COREY (*taking Nurse Pepper's case*) I'll see you later.

(COREY *exits* L. NURSE PEPPER *moves above the desk*)

LANE (*putting his cigarette in the desk ashtray*) I'd like to look in on Ellen, if I may.

KAREN. By all means. Come with me.

(KAREN *and* LANE *move* R. *Automatically* NURSE PEPPER *moves to the ashtray, hesitating as she decides it is foolish to check Lane's brand. However, she changes her mind and picks up the ashtray. Her eyes widen as she studies the butt.* KAREN *turns and sees her.*)

Nurse! (*Moving to Nurse*) I'll empty that ashtray!

NURSE PEPPER (*putting the ashtray behind her back*) Why, Mrs Clayton?

KAREN. Give it to me at once!

LANE. What is it, Karen? What's the matter?

NURSE PEPPER (*moving away* L) Doctor Lane, when did you say you got back?

LANE (*to Karen*) What's she talking about?

KAREN. The slip. I told you there would be one!

NURSE PEPPER. This cigarette, Doctor. That's what I'm talking about. It's the same brand.

KAREN. Ridiculous! Thousands of people smoke that brand.

NURSE PEPPER. Not in this country, they don't. (*To Lane, excitedly*) I thought they were American. But, of course, they're French cigarettes!

LANE (*crossing below Karen to Nurse Pepper*) I'm afraid my smoking habits are none of your business.

NURSE PEPPER. Yesterday afternoon—when I went down to the beach, you were behind me, weren't you? You were the man I saw in the window!

LANE (*after a pause; easily*) Yes, Nurse—I was.

KAREN. Paul!

(NURSE PEPPER *takes a step to the french windows and calls*)

NURSE PEPPER. Doctor Phillips!

LANE (*taking Nurse Pepper by the arms; firmly*) Easy does it, Nurse. Be quiet and nothing will happen to you.

NURSE PEPPER (*in a whisper*) You—you were here last night, too, weren't you? It was you who came up from the ledge.

(LANE *nods slowly*)

And then you went into that secret passage. Why, it must have been you who . . . (*She turns towards the french windows and screams loudly*) Doctor Phillips, come back!

LANE (*pulling her away* C, *holding her tight*) Be quiet, I said. Besides, he won't help you.

NURSE PEPPER. Of course he will!

KAREN. No—he won't.

NURSE PEPPER. I'd like to know why not!

LANE. Then I shall tell you . . . (*His hold tightens*) You see, the man who went out of here is *not* Doctor Phillips.

NURSE PEPPER (*drawing back; stunned*) He—he isn't . . . ? (*Rallying*) Oh, what are you talking about? You killed Jenny and you're making up some insane story to . . .

LANE. If I killed Jenny I wouldn't bother making up stories. (*Levelly*) I should simply send you off to join her.

(KAREN *crosses above them to the french windows*)

NURSE PEPPER. Thanks ever so but that's one trip even I don't want to take. (*Trying to pull free*) Let go of me! (*As she recalls the line in the book*) You can't get away with this. The place is surrounded!

KAREN (*looking out through the french windows*) Oh, no, it isn't. (*To* Lane) He's driven off.

LANE (*releasing Nurse Pepper*) Sorry if I bruised you but you might have spoiled everything.

(KAREN *moves behind the desk*)

NURSE PEPPER (*irately*) I still intend to! If you aren't the murderer why did you follow me down the Gap?

LANE. To protect you, Nurse.

NURSE PEPPER. Protect me! (*She sits in the chair* LC) A likely story. (*Rubbing her wrists*) Feed me to the gulls, that's what you wanted to do.

LANE (*moving* R *of Nurse Pepper*) I think you'd better listen carefully. I came here yesterday afternoon. I had just returned from France. I was about to come in from the driveway when I saw and overheard the man who pretends to be Doctor Phillips. I listened outside a few seconds and then went around to see Mrs Clayton, ask her if she knew what it was all about. Jenny let me in.

NURSE PEPPER (*suspiciously*) Oh, so Jenny knew you were back.

LANE. She took me in to see Mrs Clayton. Perhaps she listened outside the door. Anyway, I'm certain she heard me telling Mrs Clayton that the young man was not Doctor Phillips.

NURSE PEPPER. And you think Jenny confronted him and he killed her? Oh, it's preposterous.

KAREN. We think that is *one* of the reasons Jenny was killed.

NURSE PEPPER. But you said you'd never met Doctor Phillips! Only spoken to him on the phone.

LANE. I'd never met him. But I'd *seen* him.

NURSE PEPPER. Then if this man's an imposter, why didn't you go straight to the police!

LANE. Because I think there is more involved than a mere impersonation. However Mrs Clayton wants to be positive—because of Ellen.

NURSE PEPPER. Ellen? You don't think she's mixed up in this, too?

KAREN (*unhappily*) Doctor Lane is convinced she is.

NURSE PEPPER (*scoffing*) Oh—incredible. I'd as soon suspect myself.

KAREN. I couldn't believe it, either. However this man who claims to be Doctor Phillips is really the young man she was in love with in Paris.

NURSE PEPPER. The one who got into trouble?

(KAREN *nods*)

Are—are you sure?

KAREN. I can prove it. (*Taking a large leather-bound book from a drawer in the desk*) This book is the one Jenny took to her room last night. Evidently the same idea had occurred to her. You see, it's a collection of snapshots Ellen had taken in France. (*Opening the book and indicating a photo*) Here he is.

NURSE PEPPER (*after a long look*) Oh—oh, it proves nothing. They know how you feel about him. This little masquerade is just so they can be together.

KAREN. I wish it were! But Doctor Lane has even doubted for some time that Ellen is unable to walk.

NURSE PEPPER. I don't believe it! Don't you believe it either, Mrs Clayton. There'd be no point in shamming. (*To Lane*) You said her illness was psychosomatic!

LANE. I also said I was mystified. There's no proof of any paralysis. She could be faking.

NURSE PEPPER. For heaven's sake, why? She was injured in the accident and . . .

LANE. Was it an accident, Nurse Pepper?

NURSE PEPPER (*aghast*) You—you can't possibly mean . . . ? No, she wouldn't. Her own father!

LANE. She and her father quarrelled bitterly over this man. And then suddenly she gave in to him, supposedly shut the chap out of her life. Then there's the matter of the will. Does it seem credible that a man like John Clayton would neglect to make a new one!

NURSE PEPPER. No—no, it doesn't. But I still refuse to believe that Miss Ellen . . . No, I just can't!

KAREN. Ellen gave Jenny a cheque for a large amount. I don't know how many other cheques there have been. She said it was for charity.

NURSE PEPPER. It could have been!

LANE. It also could have been blackmail.

NURSE PEPPER (*rising and crossing below the sofa*) You're building up a case and it's all circumstantial. This isn't justice! And that nice young man, why just the shape of his head proves how wrong you are.

LANE (*moving L of the sofa*) I think any criminologist will assure you a good bone structure can conceal bad tendencies. As I've had to remind Karen, this man has a criminal record.

NURSE PEPPER. And any expert will assure you a lot of innocent people go to prison!

LANE. This morning I was at Briars. I couldn't let him see me. But I managed to learn he's packed up for a get-away. He also was on the phone to Dover. He's chartered a boat called *The Saturn* for a Channel crossing tonight.

NURSE PEPPER. Eloping! That's what they're doing.

LANE. A strange time to elope. The police have ordered everyone to stay for the inquest.

NURSE PEPPER. But—but if he isn't Doctor Phillips, where is the real doctor?

LANE. That's what I'm leading up to. (*With a nod toward the water*) The man said to have been accidentally drowned, couldn't he be the real doctor? Especially since he's been shot to death.

NURSE PEPPER (*horrified*) Another murder!

LANE. The hospital authorities are on their way over here now. They're going to view the body. If they identify the man as the real Phillips, I'll tell the police all my suspicions and what I actually know.

NURSE PEPPER. All you *know* is that he's been impersonating somebody else. Perhaps only to be near Miss Ellen!

LANE. Your loyalty is touching—if, I fear, misplaced.

KAREN (*moving above the desk to L of Lane*) Please, Paul! If you're going into the village, hurry. Nurse Pepper *could* be right.

LANE (*moving below the desk to the french windows*) I'll be quick as possible. I wonder . . . perhaps you two should come with me.

NURSE PEPPER. *I'm* not afraid. Not of *them*.

KAREN. I have the gun, Paul.

LANE. Then promise you won't hesitate to use it.

(KAREN *nods.* LANE *exits* L)

NURSE PEPPER (*deliberately*) Doctor Lane is most concerned about you, isn't he, Mrs Clayton?

KAREN (*sitting* LC) Naturally we've become friends. But that's all.

NURSE PEPPER (*moving* C) If you ask me his nasty suspicions could be wounded pride. Because he hasn't been able to cure Miss Ellen. I'm sure there's a nice, harmless explanation. Just a sort of youthful prank like—like . . .

KAREN (*drily*) Like setting fire to Westminster Abbey. (*Soberly*) It isn't for me to think these things. Ellen means a lot to me. I'd given up my career. I was willing to devote my life to her until she got well. But evidently this man controls her like a puppet.

NURSE PEPPER (*sitting on the* L *arm of the sofa*) Then why didn't they just go ahead and get married? Why this dreadful scheming? Why murder? (*Hastily*) That is, if they *are* guilty?

KAREN. I don't know. Unless it has something to do with money. But Ellen *has* all the money she could ever need.

NURSE PEPPER. Money. Money. Maybe millions? Could that be it?

KAREN. I scarcely think my husband left millions. He was not that kind of a lawyer.

NURSE PEPPER (*desperately*) Oh, why did she always talk in riddles!

KAREN. Who? Whom do you mean?

NURSE PEPPER (*after a second of uncertainty*) Jenny.

KAREN. Jenny! Nurse, did she tell you something?

(NURSE PEPPER *hesitates*)

Please! What did she say?

NURSE PEPPER (*rising*) Well—it didn't make too much sense but it must have meant something. I didn't know whom it was safe to tell. Not even the police. The person who killed her might find out —and understand.

KAREN. Tell me, what did she say?

NURSE PEPPER. I hope I'm doing the right thing. (*She takes a deep breath*) Well, she said—so faintly I could hardly make it out—"four million". That and no more.

KAREN. Four . . . ? What could it mean?

NURSE PEPPER. I hardly think it's the size of her estate. Unless she had a business on the side.

KAREN. I can't figure it out. Before that—you and she were in here talking—did she say anything that would tie up with *four million*.

NURSE PEPPER. No. She did say she wanted a book. But she called them her friends, said they kept secrets . . . (*Realizing, excitedly*) Secrets! *Book!* That could be it! (*Rushing over to the bookcase*) The Four Million! Are these arranged alphabetically?

KAREN. Yes. By titles.

NURSE PEPPER. Then it will be under F. Where is F? (*She searches and then looks up at the top shelf in disgust*) Naturally way up there!

(*She pulls the library stool over and stands on it*) Knowing Jenny she'd keep her secrets in the most unlikely place! (*Reading the titles intently*) It *should* be among these . . . (*Disappointedly*) No, it's not here! (*She steps off the stool*)

KAREN. I really don't know if John had a copy or not. Jenny might have put it in her room somewhere.

NURSE PEPPER. Not very likely—if she thought somebody was after it.

KAREN. Good try, anyway . . . (*Sharply*) Wait! It was on the desk the other day. Of course we have a copy! I was about to put it back when I was interrupted. (*Hurrying to the bookcase*) It's over here. I just put it on the nearest shelf. (*She looks on lower shelves and finally locates it*) Yes, here we are! (*Taking the book over to the desk*) You think there may be a clue in here?

NURSE PEPPER (*following to R of Karen*) I think she might have hidden something in it!

(KAREN *riffles through the book, then holds it up and shakes it*)

Empty! And I was almost sure . . .

(KAREN *throws the book down on the desk*)

Look, the cover! (*She picks up the book and examines the cover*) See, this binding. It's slit across the top but the book isn't at all worn. (*She feels between the binding and the cover*) Yes, there's something in here. (*Jubilantly she brings out a folded sheet of paper*) Mrs Clayton, I think the idea has paid off. (*Looking at the paper*) It's just a few lines. Addressed to all those present. Well, that's us!

KAREN (*taking it from her and scanning it hurriedly*) It's a will! It's dated May nineteenth. That was the day John was killed. And it's witnessed by Jenny and Mrs Meigs.

NURSE PEPPER. And Mrs Meigs died soon after. So only Jenny knew about it. She wanted to protect Miss Ellen but didn't have the courage to destroy it.

KAREN (*thoughtfully*) She might have been holding it over Ellen's head. Perhaps that is why Ellen was giving her money.

NURSE PEPPER. I don't think anything of the sort!

KAREN (*reading the will*) Especially since practically everything is left to me, if she *marries* him, that is. (*Determinedly*) I'm going after Doctor Lane. Then we'll take this to the police. (*She moves L*)

NURSE PEPPER. Wait, please. (*She draws Karen back to up C*) If the poor child is innocent don't you realize the harm this will do to her?

KAREN (*with difficulty*) I can hardly believe she's innocent. Not now.

NURSE PEPPER (*imploringly*) She's innocent until proven guilty. And when she discovers the awful things you're accusing her of, she'll *never* walk again.

KAREN. If she isn't already walking! (*Relenting*) Oh—all right, what do you suggest we do?

NURSE PEPPER. When I have faith in someone I'll go down with my flag flying. No matter what I have to do to back myself up. Now there must be some way to . . . (*She snaps her fingers*) But of course! It's as simple as that. (*She crosses below Karen to the desk*)

KAREN. What are you going to do?

NURSE PEPPER. Determine if she's running away with him by checking with *The Saturn* at Dover. Certainly the captain will know how many passengers he's taking across.

KAREN. Be careful. There are extensions in the house.

NURSE PEPPER (*lifting the receiver*) Then all we can do is pray she isn't listening. If she *is* mixed up in murder. (*Into the phone*) Hello . . . Will you please see if you can get me the . . .

(COREY *enters suddenly through the french windows.* NURSE PEPPER *almost drops the receiver as she sees him. She manages a weak smile and hangs up*)

Why—why, Doctor Phillips. Back so soon?

COREY. It was just a simple errand. Don't let me interrupt your call.

NURSE PEPPER (*backing upstage a pace*) There's no point in my making the call. I just remembered it's Cousin Maude's time. She'll be in hospital. Her fourth. Some people never get tired.

COREY (*crossing R below Karen and Nurse Pepper*) I suppose Ellen's about ready.

KAREN. I believe she is.

COREY. I'll go see.

(COREY *gives a speculative look toward* NURSE PEPPER, *who stands by the phone with elaborate innocence.* COREY *exits* R)

NURSE PEPPER (*moving* C) That was a close one! (*A loud whisper*) I don't dare call from here now. How far is the nearest phone?

KAREN. About a mile down the road.

NURSE PEPPER. Good. Now shall we break a speed record?

KAREN. Nurse, whatever you're up to, we're wasting time!

NURSE PEPPER. It's worth it to spare Miss Ellen. To prove I'm right.

KAREN (*reluctantly*) Very well, a few more minutes can't matter.

NURSE PEPPER (*moving to the french windows*) Then for goodness' sake let's hurry. (*Looking towards the hallway*) I hope it's all right to leave her.

KAREN (*going to the desk and opening the drawer for the gun*) I'm afraid you needn't worry about my step-daughter.

(NURSE PEPPER *hurries out* L. KAREN *takes the gun from the drawer and exits after Nurse Pepper. The stage is deserted. The sky outside becomes darker. Gulls break the ominous quiet as a minute passes.* ELLEN *appears in the hallway and wheels herself into the room. She is pale and tense showing the strain she is under. She looks round enquiringly, then wheels herself to the french windows and calls)*

ELLEN. Karen! Nurse! (*Perplexed and nervous, she turns, takes a cigarette from a packet in her lap and looks for matches. Unable to find any, she looks at the lighter on the desk, hesitates, then wheels herself towards it. Somewhere in the house a door is slammed. She gives a start, and looks towards the hallway*) Who—who's there? (*Wheeling herself above the desk to* LC) Who is it? Answer me! (*Frightened, she waits, then wheels herself* C. *She glances at the french windows as though tempted to flee. At a sound from the hallway, she gasps with relief*) Oh, darling!

(COREY *enters* R)

I'm so glad it's you.

COREY (*moving to* R *of Ellen*) Ellen dearest, what is it?

ELLEN. I heard a noise. I was terrified. I didn't know you'd come back.

COREY. I just got here. What happened to the others?

ELLEN. I saw Karen's car taking off. Strange, if they've gone without saying anything.

COREY. Yes—damned strange.

ELLEN. That noise I heard before—where were you?

COREY (*with a sheepish grin*) Might as well confess. I was in Jenny's room, playing detective. I thought I might find some shred of evidence.

ELLEN. Surely the police went over every inch.

COREY. You can't blame a chap for trying. They might have missed something.

ELLEN. I couldn't go into her room. Poor Jenny, it's such a night-mare. Who could have stabbed her?

COREY. Undoubtedly the same person who set my car afire. Who wanted to kill me—or us. You know whom I suspect.

ELLEN. And I know you're wrong!

COREY. Oh well, from now on we'll have nothing to worry about. (*Taking a large legal type envelope from his pocket*) I had the contract drawn. And the cheque made out. (*He takes a cheque from his wallet and replaces the envelope*) All it needs is your signature.

ELLEN. It—it seems such a lot of money to draw out at once.

COREY. Darling, you'll get it back ten times over. It's a damned sound investment.

ELLEN. I suppose if you're sure . . .

COREY (*taking her hand*) Of course I'm sure. It's a spot of Cornwall I know so well. Used to go there when I was a kid. And the hotel is in tip-top shape. It's worth every penny. Oh, it's going to be hard work, running it. But together we'll swing it.

ELLEN. I don't know how much of a help I'll be.

COREY. I thought you weren't going to talk that way! New scenery, activity, our marriage—Ellen, it's exactly what you've wanted. (*Handing the cheque to her*) Now sign this. We'll stop at the bank and get the money.

ELLEN (*leaning her head against him as he stands beside her*) I am so much better since you came. Everything's changed. I feel a little like my old self again.

COREY. I knew you would. That's why I refused to stay away— as you begged me to. (*Kissing the top of her head*) Perhaps I'm a bit of a doctor after all.

ELLEN (*appealingly*) We can tell them the truth now, can't we?

COREY. Why not? Besides, now that Lane is back they'll find out. I think he'll understand. I had to be near you and there was no other way. Not with the wicked stepmother standing guard.

ELLEN. It isn't Karen's fault. She simply believed what father said about you.

COREY. I don't care what she thinks of me. You know what I think of her. I tell you, Ellen, it's a good thing I came here. Both your sanity and your safety were in danger.

ELLEN. No. She wants me to get well, to be happy.

COREY (*with a dry laugh*) With a fortune falling into her lap if anything should happen to you? You've always had money, my girl. You don't know what it can mean to those who haven't. What they'd do to get their hands on some. (*Indicating the porch*) I don't want to alarm you but why was she constantly telling people you threatened suicide? I don't know for sure but I think she had a card up her sleeve. (*Wheeling her to the desk*) But we don't have to worry about her now.

ELLEN (*picking up the pen, then pausing*) Darling, I should so like to meet the real Doctor Phillips.

COREY. He's anxious to meet you, too. He has romantic problems of his own, so he understands.

ELLEN. The coincidence, his having gone to school with you!

COREY. Imagine my luck, having kept in touch with him. One of the few chaps I have. (*Urgently*) Now if we want to get to the bank before it closes . . .

ELLEN. Why do we have to give them cash?

COREY. I've explained all that. There are other bidders. It's the first with the cash who closes the deal.

ELLEN (*doubtfully*) Couldn't we wait just a day or so? I don't feel well. My mind is confused. And I know so little about . . .

COREY. Ellen, I've investigated the proposition from every angle! Good Lord, don't you trust me?

ELLEN. Darling, you know I do. It's only that . . .

COREY. And you love me? We *are* going to be married?

ELLEN. Love you? I love you so much I feel guilty allowing you to tie yourself to anyone like me.

COREY. Tie . . . ? You're being foolish again. You'll be walking soon. Of course you will. Once we're together and away from here! ELLEN. I'm—I'm a very lucky girl.

(ELLEN *starts to sign the cheque as the telephone rings. She looks at it, hesitates, but finishes her signature before picking it up*)

Hello . . . Yes . . . It's who? (*To Corey, her hand over the mouthpiece*) Such an odd voice. (*Into the phone*) . . . Yes, but don't you want to talk to him? . . . Very well, what is the message? (*She listens*) Are you sure you have the right number? . . . Yes, I'll give Doctor Phillips the message. (*She looks up at Corey in shocked disbelief*)

(COREY *stares back at her, then whips the receiver from her hand*)

COREY. Hello, who is it? . . . Hello! . . . They've rung off. (*Replacing the receiver*) Ellen, who was it? What was the message?
ELLEN (*still looking into his eyes, in a low voice*) It was from Dover. Due to weather conditions Captain Gray has cancelled the Channel crossing until seven tomorrow morning.
COREY (*after a stunned second, rallies*) Channel crossing? Why, there's a mistake. I'm not crossing the . . .
ELLEN. Aren't you?
COREY. Someone's playing a joke!
ELLEN. Then—then shall we call back and find out? (*She reaches slowly for the phone*)
COREY (*taking the phone from her*) Don't be ridiculous, darling. It's another Phillips. Of course, it's the *real* Phillips!
ELLEN. Why would he give this number? (*Watching him closely*) Why—why don't you want me to check back?
COREY. For the simple reason I think you should trust me.
ELLEN. Is this the reason you were so anxious to have me sign the cheque? Why we were going to the bank? Corey, would I ever see you again after you went *into* the bank?
COREY. Ellen, you *are* upset. I've never seen you like this. My darling, that phone call was a joke, I tell you. (*His arms around her*) Dearest, what's the matter with you?
ELLEN (*with a shrill laugh*) I'm beginning to wonder. You see, there's something else I've got to ask you. Something I tried to shut out of my mind. Why did you tell the police you didn't come back into the house last night? After you put me in the car?
COREY. Why—why, it's obvious why I didn't. Why should I get involved over nothing? I only brought your chair back in.
ELLEN. You were gone quite some time!
COREY. I—I had to get cigarettes!
ELLEN. Where did you get them?
COREY. I came in here. Got some from Nurse Pepper.
ELLEN. Nurse Pepper doesn't smoke.

COREY. Darling, I didn't say she did. There was a packet on the desk.

ELLEN. *She* didn't tell the police you came back in either.

COREY. Of course not. She knew it was of no importance! Ellen, why this third degree?

ELLEN (*almost hysterical*) Please—*please* look at me and tell me you had nothing to do with Jenny's death! *Can* you look at me and tell me . . . ?

COREY. I had nothing to do with it. You're overwrought, hysterical. Now I don't want to hear any more. (*He moves* R) I'll get your coat and things and . . .

ELLEN. I'm not going to the bank.

(COREY *turns, looks at her and then at the cheque on the desk. Her eyes follow his gaze. She starts to reach for the cheque but he is there, his hand on it. He picks it up. Their eyes meet: hers with final realization, his with a slow smile*)

COREY (*quietly*) It's been quite an education for you, hasn't it? Now you know that some people will do anything, I repeat *anything* for money.

ELLEN. You never planned to marry me at all. It was just to get the money . . .

COREY. Oh, I planned to marry you. That is, up until last night. I was playing for really high stakes. Then Jenny descended upon me, told me to go away. Said you wouldn't get a cent if you married me. It seems, my dear, there's another will tucked away some place. Jenny hid it because she didn't want Karen to get any of your father's money.

ELLEN. Jenny knew your real identity?

COREY. Somehow she found out yesterday afternoon. She said that if the saintly John Clayton didn't like me I must really be a bounder. When she threatened to produce the new will I told her I'd make the supreme sacrifice and vanish from your life. However last night when I returned with your chair I pulled the master fuse and killed her when she came to investigate. I left her in the cellar for dead. But somehow she managed to climb up that passage-way.

ELLEN. And—and the real Doctor Phillips? What about him?

COREY (*shaking his head*) Only a girl in love would have swallowed that tale. The day he arrived at Briars I was waiting for him. He must have been quite surprised at the welcome—if he ever came to.

ELLEN. The car! Why did you set fire to the car?

COREY. To remove suspicion. All along I'd been building up a case against Karen. Nobody knew about the new will. Karen had motive enough—since you were leaving everything to her. As we got out of that car I lighted that cloth. It served as a fuse. (*Looking at the cheque*) Well, I'd expected to marry you and get it all but this will tide me over for a while.

ELLEN. I'll stop payment! (*Reaching for the telephone*) I'll call the bank and . . .

COREY. Oh, no, you don't! (*He grabs the telephone from her hand, crosses above her to the wall L and rips out the cord*)

ELLEN (*sinking weakly back into her chair*) What are you going to do?

COREY. Unfortunately for you I've a strong instinct of self-preservation. And since you know too much . . .

ELLEN. You're going to kill me, of course. (*She wheels herself to* C) All right, go ahead. As though I cared. I can't walk. I can't do anything. I might as well be dead. You were all I had. My love for you and the love I thought you felt for me. There's nothing to live for now. Go ahead and kill me. I don't care!

COREY (*wryly*) Fortunately you've advertised that fact. Poor little Ellen, the girl who wanted to die. Therefore no-one will be surprised. (*With a mock sigh*) I supposed I cared as much for you as I could for anybody. You were rich and you were beautiful. In that order. (*Putting the cheque away*) Perhaps some day in Europe or South America or even the States, they'll pick me up. But what can they prove? Even this cheque—well, you loved me and since you planned to kill yourself, you wanted to leave me something to remember you by. (*He moves towards her*)

ELLEN (*wheeling herself* RC; *with a great effort*) No . . . ! No, they're not going to think that! I'm not going to let you get away with it. You're too horrible. I can't let you . . . (*She struggles to get out of the chair*)

COREY (*holding the chair and speaking softly, with exaggerated sympathy*) So much determination. But so late . . .

(ELLEN *struggles in vain and falls back exhausted in her chair. He goes to the porch, steps out and opens the gate. It sways in the wind. She turns, watches, and understands what he plans to do. She summons enough strength to wheel herself towards the french windows. He sees her, moves quickly to her side and grabs the chair. He turns it around rapidly, almost throws it towards the porch. She is still struggling, half-rising from the chair as* NURSE PEPPER *rushes in through the french windows*)

NURSE PEPPER. Miss Ellen!!

COREY (*turning swiftly*) What the devil! I thought you'd gone!

NURSE PEPPER. I had—but only to the neighbour's. Now get away from her. Quickly now. And don't try any shennanigans. (*She pulls the gun from her pocket, holding it unsteadily as she points it at him*) I've never fired one of these but I'll try anything once. (*With concern*) You all right, Miss Ellen? I came back as soon as I found out.

COREY. How'd you find out?

NURSE PEPPER. A simple bluff. I didn't even bother to verify with Dover. I knew Miss Ellen couldn't have been planning to elope anywhere with you. You see, I'd helped her pack. And no girl elopes with a flannel nightgown!

ELLEN. I—I don't understand.

NURSE PEPPER. I had to let you know that he'd chartered a boat. So I disguised my voice and called here.

COREY. That was *you?*

NURSE PEPPER. Doing my impersonation of Donald Duck. This poor lovesick girl never would have taken the word of Nurse Pepper!

COREY (*stepping away from Ellen*) It seems I should have got rid of you the day I shot at you. And deliberately missed.

NURSE PEPPER. Thanks for small favours. Now stand still, young man! If *I* miss it won't be deliberate.

COREY. That *is* Mrs Clayton's gun?

NURSE PEPPER. Yes. (*She moves up* LC) She gave it to me when she stayed behind to make more phone calls. The police, the coastguard, the ambulance. (*Warningly*) The latter just in case . . .

COREY. Her gun. I suspected as much. (*He takes a step towards the french windows*)

NURSE PEPPER. Stand still! Just because it's her gun doesn't mean it won't shoot.

COREY. Oh, but it does, Nurse. You see, I removed the bullets this morning.

NURSE PEPPER. Wha . . . ? Oh, as though I'd believe anything you'd say!

COREY. And since I intend to make a break for it . . .

NURSE PEPPER (*nervously*) Will you stand still! I can't let you get away to go on killing . . .

COREY (*running round below the desk to the french windows*) That gun is empty. Not that you'd shoot anyway.

NURSE PEPPER (*in desperation, trying it once again in ringing tones*) You can't get away with it. The place is surrounded!

COREY. Ha! (*About to run out, he draws back*) My God, it is!

NURSE PEPPER (*astonished*) It is?

(COREY *runs back below the desk to* R)

(*Recovering and taking aim*) I'm—I'm warning you. You stay here.

(COREY *continues* R, *running below the sofa on his way to the hall.* NURSE PEPPER *closes her eyes and fires. There is a sharp report*)

ELLEN (*screaming and looking away*) Nurse . . . !

(COREY *clutches his left arm, takes a few steps and dazedly reaches for the sofa*)

You've—you've killed him. (*She struggles to rise*)

NURSE PEPPER (*opening her eyes*) I have?

(COREY *sinks on to the sofa*)

No, he's just winged. (*She crosses below the desk to* L *of Corey*) You said it wasn't loaded, young man. This will teach you not to lie.

(ELLEN *manages to rise from the chair and take a few paces down stage to* L *of Nurse Pepper*)

Miss Ellen!

ELLEN (*realizing; joyfully*) Nurse, I—I'm walking. (*Half laughing, half crying*) I can walk! (*She continues walking to Nurse Pepper, each step more sure*)

NURSE PEPPER. Miss Ellen, you are. Oh, my dear, you are! (*She takes Ellen in her arms and embraces her happily*)

KAREN *and* DOCTOR LANE *hurry in through the french windows, as—*

the CURTAIN *falls*

FURNITURE AND PROPERTY LIST

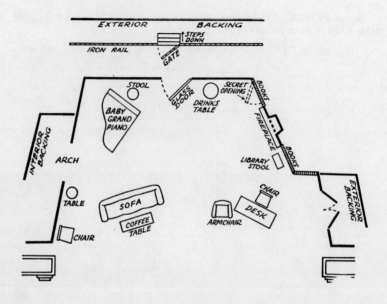

ACT I

SCENE I

On stage: Sofa (RC) *On it:* cushions
Small armchair (LC)
Desk chair
Small upright chair (down R)
Coffee-table (below sofa) *On it:* ashtray, Doctor Lane's valise, cigarette box, lighter
Small table (R) *On it:* vase (to be broken)
Desk (LC) *On it:* writing materials, pen, telephone (upstage end), ashtray, lighter, scissors. *In drawers:* torch, pistol, package of bullets
Library stool
Baby grand piano (up R)
Piano stool

Drinks table (up LC) *On it:* sherry, whisky, gin, brandy, martini, gin, tonic water, bottle-opener, lemonade, glasses, cocktail-shaker, field-glasses

In bookshelves: books on all shelves, including one large leather-bound volume

On mantelpiece: candles in candlesticks, matches, clock, vase

Over mantelpiece: portrait of John Clayton

Carpet

Window curtains

Off stage: Wheel-chair and blankets (ELLEN)
Newspapers and magazines (JENNY)
Bunch of flowers (KAREN)
Two suitcases and umbrella (NURSE PEPPER)
Wool scarf (JENNY)

Personal: NURSE PEPPER: handbag with paper-back thriller

SCENE 2

Strike: Flower stalks from desk

Off stage: Newspaper (JENNY)
Book (JENNY)
Bowl of ice (JENNY)
Doctor's bag (COREY)

Personal: NURSE PEPPER: watch, pack of cards

ACT II

SCENE 1

Strike: Dirty glasses

Set: Shaker back on drinks table
Newspaper on desk

Off stage: Letters, including bank statement and cheques (JENNY)
Bills, cheque-book (KAREN)
Bottle of pills and tumbler of water (NURSE PEPPER)
Doctor's bag (COREY)
Bowl of flowers (JENNY)

Personal: NURSE PEPPER: paper-back thriller, pack of cards

SCENE 2

Strike: Bills and letters from desk
Pills and tumbler

Off stage: Green leaf (LANE)
Torch (COREY)

Personal: NURSE PEPPER: handkerchief wrapped round half-smoked
cigarette, pack of cards

ACT III

Strike: Playing cards
Brandy glass

Set: Large leather-bound book in desk drawer
Cushion back on sofa
Pistol back in desk drawer

Check: Sheet of paper in binding of book in bookshelves

Off stage: Bed-sheets (NURSE PEPPER)
Green leaf (from previous scene) (COREY)
Two suitcases (COREY)
Packet of cigarettes (ELLEN)
Large legal envelope with contract (COREY)

Personal: LANE: cigarette case, full
COREY: wallet with cheque

LIGHTING PLOT

Property fittings required: wall- and fire-brackets
    Interior. A sitting-room. The same scene throughout
    THE APPARENT SOURCES OF LIGHT are: by day, glass doors up C and
    french windows L; by night, brackets
    THE MAIN ACTING AREAS are RC, down RC, up C, C, up LC, LC, L

ACT I, SCENE 1. Afternoon

To open: Effect of September afternoon light
No cues

ACT I, SCENE 2. Afternoon

To open: Effect of late afternoon light
No cues

ACT II, SCENE 1. Afternoon

To open: Effect of grey afternoon
Cue 1   NURSE PEPPER exits   (Page 36)
          Fade daylight to half

ACT II, SCENE 2. Night

To open: Brackets on
         Blue outside windows

Cue 2   NURSE PEPPER resumes her solitaire   (Page 43)
          Black-out on stage

Cue 3   KAREN lights candles   (Page 44)
          Bring up covering Spots

Cue 4   NURSE PEPPER: ". . . what was that?"   (Page 47)
          Red flickering glow off L

ACT III. Afternoon

To open: Effect of dull afternoon light
Cue 5   KAREN exits   (Page 60)
          Fade daylight to half

EFFECTS PLOT

ACT I

SCENE 1

No cues

SCENE 2

Cue 1	JENNY crosses to desk *Gunshots*	(Page 13)
Cue 2	NURSE PEPPER shuffles cards *Telephone rings*	(Page 22)
Cue 3	NURSE PEPPER replaces receiver *Sea-gulls, followed by gunshot and breaking vase*	(Page 22)

ACT II

SCENE 1

Cue 4	On CURTAIN up *Sea-gulls*	(Page 24)
Cue 5	NURSE PEPPER: ". . . it was the wind" *Thunder*	(Page 24)
Cue 6	ELLEN: ". . . but it can wait" *Thunder*	(Page 25)
Cue 7	NURSE PEPPER: ". . . to the Underground" *Sea-gulls*	(Page 33)
Cue 8	KAREN: ". . . quite late, you know" *Gulls quiet*	(Page 33)
Cue 9	NURSE PEPPER moves R *Thunder*	(Page 36)
Cue 10	NURSE PEPPER exits *Thunder*	(Page 36)
Cue 11	LANE exits *Thunder*	(Page 36)

SCENE 2

Cue 12	KAREN: *"Murder"* *Explosion*	(Page 46)

ACT III

Cue 13	As CURTAIN rises *Sea-gulls*	(Page 48)
Cue 14	After KAREN exits *Sea-gulls*	(Page 60)
Cue 15	ELLEN starts to sign cheque *Telephone rings*	(Page 63)

MADE AND PRINTED IN GREAT BRITAIN BY
WHITSTABLE LITHO LTD., WHITSTABLE, KENT